I wish I had known

Jenny,

I enjoyed your reflections today, very well structured and insightful. I hope you discover new ways to progress in your career and "be selfish" to take care of yourself.

I look forward to your feedback and hearing about your book!

Susanne.

Susana Serrano-Davey

I WISH
I HAD
KNOWN

*Practical guide for your professional
development at work*

Theory, anecdotes and exercises to get you where you
want to be without overwhelming or betraying yourself

First paperback edition: november 2022

ISBN: 978-84-09-43476-3
Legal Deposit: MA-1620-2022

My thanks to all the people who, over the years, have helped me ignite the beacons of enlightenment that I can now share with you.

My recognition to my zero readers for their incalculable contribution to the final result and for the opportunity to put into practice what this book is really all about.

My love to John for always being such an unconditional supporter through all the stages of our life journey.

INDEX

This guide will help you reach your full potential, whilst taking care of your personal self. This section will tell you about the methodology that we will follow to increase your skills and widen your perspectives in order to enrich your work career and journey of personal discovery.

PART ONE

The outside world:

Environment: **Understanding how your organisation and relationships work is the basis for improving your skills and your position in any company.**

"One night I came home from a work event and when I got into bed with my husband I said, 'Darling, I just discovered the secret of how to climb the career ladder...'"

- Four elements to consider to improve your relationships.
  - Analyse your environment.

"Suddenly, my eyes widened like saucers as I stared at him with a forced smile."

- Some ways to mitigate conflict, and even take advantage of them.
  - ✎ Could you now know how to manage your last conflict better?

3 - Others can be of great help 61

"I had power-dressed for the occasion, determined to be unfazed by doubts or objections ..."

- The keys to obtain consensus.
  - ✎ Prepare the next change you want to promote in your company.
- Shared decisions.
- Asking for help works.
  - ✎ Reflect on your previous experiences.
- Mentors and allies.
  - ✎ Analyse the advantages of mentoring.
  - ✎ Find your potential allies.

4 - Take the reins 79

"When I learned how to apply them and took the initiative unapologetically, I saw that there was no secret."

- Promote yourself, without arrogance but with conviction.
  - ✎ Develop your personal value proposition.
- Four steps to balance the relationship with your direct manager.
  - ✎ Evaluate to correct your current situation.
- The points you must take care of to be one step ahead.
  - ✎ Reflect on a previous experience and how you could have benefited from better information.
  - ✎ Let's discuss the causes of, and solutions to, those meetings where you feel frustration.

Development: **Embrace change! Doing so will sharpen your skills to handle and take advantage of the situations that will arise.**

5 - Change is the way

"And Heraclitus said: The only thing that is constant is change."

- Identify the types, listen to your instinct and make decisions.
- Make it happen, look ahead and decide how and who to involve.
- Save your objections, curb your enthusiasm - and a few more things you should take care of.
  - ✎ Review your latest proposal for a personal or work change.
- Attitude is everything: the advantages of change.
  - ✎ Learn from the last change you've resisted and consider if you could have done better with hindsight.

6 - How we do things matters

"When working in graduate programmes, many may have brilliant academic records but their soft skills leave something to be desired which could easily be improved."

- Effective Communication: Face-to-face and in writing. Learn how to captivate your audience.
  - ✎ Evaluate your style and identify what you can improve.
  - ✎ Evaluate your written communication.
  - ✎ Let's practice with ELOISA.
- Teamwork: even a goatherd needs it!
  - ✎ Teamwork? "Yes, but ..."
- Resilience: the ability to take advantage of situations.
  - ✎ Work on your resilience and improve it.
  - ✎ Basic exercise to assess any skill.

"Dumbfounded, I ended the conversation as soon as I could and left to catch my train, utterly devastated and feeling as if the ground was shaking under my feet. That conversation..."

- Feedback: that word so overused and always neglected.
- Feedback: giving, receiving and what you should watch out for to take advantage of it more and more.
  - ✎ Three exercises for you to improve in this area.
  - ✎ We can also do it well at home.

"It was embroiled in a tense meeting with a client, one of several we had had in a matter of weeks. The atmosphere could have been cut with a knife. He was restless and impatient; his comments were curt and becoming louder as the meeting progressed..."

- The challenge: to really turn the page and keep the best part.
  - ✎ Let's work with an example, not yours, but from your surroundings.
  - ✎ And now let's do it with one of yours.

PART TWO

Your inner world:

Self: **Getting to know yourself and realising how you are perceived is an essential step towards being able to improve and reaching that ideal that you seek.**

"When my daughter phoned me in tears to tell me what she had decided, my answer was..."

- The simile of the matrioshkas and the four elements to work on self-awareness.

  ✎ Evaluate your degree of self-knowledge, and start exploring.

"This was the first step to change my perspective, manage stress and live differently ..."

- The importance of your biases and your point of view. WhatsApp: a simile and ally.

  ✎ Identify and analyse your biases (an exercise that will take you several days).

"My breathing and the beads of sweat on my forehead gave me away and another student looked at me and said, Susana, are you okay?"

- Let's put assumptions aside to consciously choose the right answer.

  ✎ At whom do you point the finger?

  ✎ Identify the bodily sensation of your impulsive responses.

  ✎ Transform your reluctance into a guide.

  ✎ Redefine the opinion you have of yourself.

"You always leave the toilet lid up," and the other thinks, "It's not true because I usually put it down." This is a mundane example of what the subconscious can generate.

- Are you sure you are the way you think?

- What we hide is not all negative: an infallible method to help you discover and take advantage of it.
  - ✎ Dig in and discover your hidden side.

Wellness: ***What a journey! Now all that is left is you, so never forget to take care of this part so you don't break along the way.***

"Emotions are there, whether we acknowledge them or not, and learning to recognise and digest them makes us feel better rather than getting stuck."

- Emotional states.
  - ✎ Observe them for 7 days and draw conclusions.
- Learn to regulate your self-esteem.
  - ✎ Regulate your self-esteem (like the Ph in a swimming pool).
- Your CRASH status is inevitable.
  - ✎ Learn how to prevent and mitigate it.

"That's how I felt that day, when what should have been one of the star moments of the year became a nightmare, with that feeling of emptiness in my stomach, knowing that I had made a mistake and wishing to disappear."

- The best ways to control and minimise those internal voices which can cause us huge chagrin if they are really invasive.
- Your torture.
  - ✎ Calm your mind to mitigate it.
  - ✎ Connect with your happy space.

- The boycotter.
  - ✎ Push back with affirmations.
- The Judge.

15 - Act coherently

"You have to get off the hamster wheel. Otherwise, we are unable to see what's on the horizon and that which is evident to others, both challenges and opportunities."

- The key question to ask and how to make a conscious choice when deciding your actions.
- Tips for when and how to get help.
- The time to let go: when and how; to avoid harming yourself.
  - ✎ Evaluate what you need, compared to the time you devote.

16 - Take care of your health

"Every Friday afternoon my jaw hurt and, when I fell asleep, it closed with such force that the noise used to wake me up."

- Stressed? Burned out? Be careful.
  - ✎ Assess your situation to get away from stress.
- Discover your harmful habits.
- Hard but simple: Take care of your habits, your body and your attitude.
  - ✎ Your formula to create regular exercise.

FIND YOUR OWN WAY

"I'm not willing to sell my life. He looked at me with surprise and repeated the phrase I had just used."

- Choose your desires again and what it means to succeed.
  - ✎ Succeeding for you is ...
  - ✎ Ponder and calculate how much it costs you.
- My last question for you.

INTRODUCTION

The workplace presents countless challenges and many learning opportunities which are not included in traditional syllabuses but are useful in our professional and personal progression — things I wish I had been told when I started out. I learned them through trial and error — my grey hairs bear witness to that — and they have led to my particular methods of addressing those challenges.

I am a consultant and mentor. After a solid career as an executive and entrepreneur, as a woman and a leader in business environments, I have faced those challenges that professionals encounter on a daily basis. These experiences have been translated into simple but, at the same time, powerful learning tools which have enabled me to see the world from different perspectives and this, in turn, has helped me achieve the things I really wanted, increasing my level of self-awareness.

The methodology I want to share with you, developed throughout my career, has added value to all areas in my life, not only at work. This book will help you to gain a broader perspective of the situations you encounter; allow you to manage both your external environment and your inner experience effectively; increase your ability to influence others through empathy and collaboration; understand yourself and safeguard your personal needs while pursuing your own work goals.

Through consulting, mentoring and training, I accompany professionals and entrepreneurs on their journeys. My objective is to help you reach your full potential at work and especially for you to take care of yourself. This guide is my way of achieving that purpose, even if we don't have the opportunity to interact face-to-face.

This book pursues its aim differently to other publications in its category. Each topic is accompanied by self-enquiry exercises which allow you to reflect on the subject from your own personal perspective so that you can gain new insights and act accordingly.

My wish is to equip you with the methodologies I have developed to succesfully manage most situations. With them, I hope that you will find a way to foster a collaborative and balanced work environment which favours your personal growth, whilst at the same time, reaping the benefits of a sustainable and enriching working life.

SHALL WE BEGIN?

Welcome to your personal development journey. During this expedition you will be able to explore your world with the tools I have designed, draw up your own map and thus define the best route towards your future in the short and medium term.

We, and the environment in which we live, are constantly developing. Our ability to adapt to these changes is vital to enable us to achieve the results we want with whatever resources we have.

The purpose of this exploration is to enrich your professional and personal development. This evolution is fundamentally based on a better understanding and management of two dimensions:

1.— OUTER WORLD

I will

ENVIRONMENT.—
Your job and work environment

DEVELOPMENT .—
Your level of ambition and development expectations

- share strategies to help you understand and successfully navigate the complex environment in which we operate.
- provide you with new perspectives to analyse that environment in all directions.
- give you the methodologies I have developed and practical tools to address the situations you face.
- facilitate your professional advancement and personal satisfaction.

2.— INNER WORLD

To increase your level of self-awareness, improve your personal well-being and work-life balance:

- identify your internal dialogue and needs as a human being.
- promote your care as a person, physically and emotionally, while developing professionally.

SELF.—
Who you are

WELL-BEING.—
Your physical and emotional state

So where does one start? Knowing where to start is part of the challenge so, to guide you along the way, we are going to break down the territory into four areas: Environment, Development, Self and Well-being.

To begin with, we will measure your level of satisfaction in these four areas. The result of this self-assessment will help you identify which areas may be interesting as a starting point or as the next steps in your development journey. This exercise will give you an indicative and intuitive measure of your degree of evolution in each of these areas.

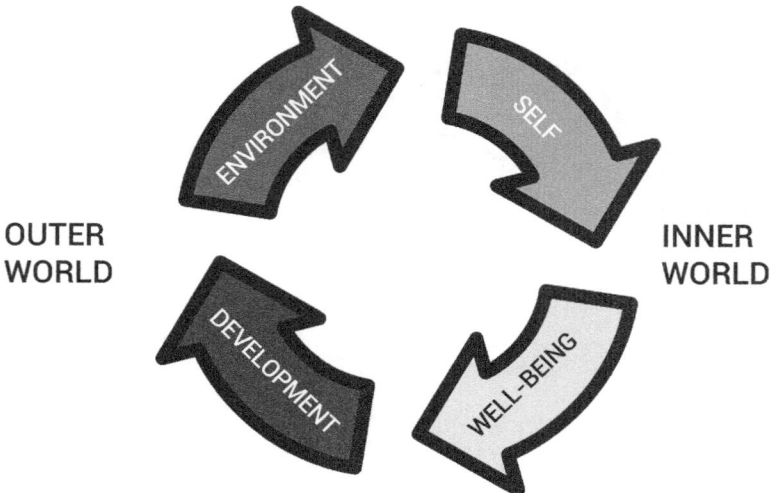

OUTER WORLD

ENVIRONMENT

SELF

DEVELOPMENT

WELL-BEING

INNER WORLD

Many of the topics covered contain exercises designed to promote reflection and self-enquiry in these areas. It is not absolutely necessary to do the exercises but in my experience they are always useful. By doing so you will get the most out of each topic, as this will put into context your own circumstances around each subject.

I'm going to share my experiences with you but, since we're all different, with that personal enquiry it will be easier for you to find your own answers. Let's start, then, with your first exercise!

Score your level of satisfaction in these four areas from 1 to 10, with 1 being "Strongly disagree" and 10 "Completely agree".

OUTER WORLD

1 ENVIRONMENT

This entails your role, the environment in which you operate and your direct line manager (if you report directly to someone or there is someone you need to please) and the team you lead.

		Score
Role	I am satisfied with my role and position at work	
	My role allows me to learn and develop	
	I have the tools and support to perform my job well	
Work environment	The environment at my workplace is good	
	I feel part of the team and know how to fit in	
Direct line manager	I am happy with my direct line manager	
	I feel valued	
	My direct manager helps me to perform my job well and grow	
Direct team (only if you are responsible for leading a team)	I feel comfortable leading a team	
	There is good communication between my team and I	
	I am satisfied with my team's performance	
	I feel I am respected by my team	
	Average	

2 DEVELOPMENT

This entails your level of ambition, soft skills and professional trajectory.

		Score
Ambition	I am an ambitious person	
	I know what my next professional step will be	
	I know where I want to be in five years	
Professional projection	I can continue to advance in my organisation	
	I am proactive with my professional development	
	I can change my job or organisation	
Soft skills	I am aware of what competencies are my strengths	
	I know what skills I need to advance my progress	
	I have opportunities to develop my soft skills	
	I know how to actively improve any competencies which can be developed	
	Average	

INNER WORLD

3 SELF

This entails your value proposition, vocation, values and beliefs.

		Score
Value proposition	I know my strengths well	
	I know my weaknesses well	
	I am aware of the aspects in which I add value to my work environment	
	I assertively convey my value proposition regularly	
Vocation	I work on what I enjoy	
	I know what aspects of my work I love	
	I know what aspects of my position I dislike	
	I enjoy doing what I do	
	If I started over, I would do the same thing	
Values	I know my values well	
	I put them into practice in my work	
	My organisation's culture supports those values	
	I can say no to situations that conflict with my values	
Beliefs	My environment is full of opportunities	
	I am a talented person	
	I am able to achieve what I set my mind to	
	Average	

4 WELL-BEING

This entails your work-life balance, health and fitness as well as your emotional well-being and stress levels.

		Score
Work-life balance	My private life does not suffer because of work	
	I do things I love outside of work	
	When I'm not working I put it out of my mind	
	I have plenty of time for my family and friends	
	I spend time alone regularly	
Health and fitness	I do some physical activity or sport regularly	
	I'm physically fit	
	I am in good health	
	I feel good about my body	
	My digestive system works like clockwork	
Stress and emotional well-being	I sleep well	
	I wake up happy in the mornings	
	I feel good during the day	
	I am in control of my life and situations	
		Average

Although you can start reading this manual at the areas where you have obtained a low score in the exercise, I personally recommend that you read it in the order presented. Paying particular attention to those areas with a lower score will, of course, help. My suggestion is that you work on aspects of both dimensions, both inner and outer.

Part one

YOUR OUTER WORLD

In this first part we will talk about:

Environment: relationships, conflict, and initiatives you can take to improve your positioning within your organisation.

Development: change, soft skills and how to integrate and learn from other perspectives.

ENVIRONMENT

Relationships, conflict, and initiatives you can take to improve your positioning within your organisation.

Chapter 1

RELATIONSHIPS MAKE ALL THE DIFFERENCE

This chapter will give you the keys to accessing the opportunities available because if you manage your interactions properly you will have influence beyond your immediate environment and enjoy the fruits of the seeds you sow.

Our environment is broad and contains many elements: the place where we live and work, culture, family, work, colleagues, and more. Your success will largely depend not only on your environment but on how you navigate it.

MUCH DEPENDS ON THE QUALITY OF OUR RELATIONSHIPS

One night I came home from a work function and when I got into bed with my husband I said, "Darling, I just discovered the secret of how to climb the career ladder. I have to go to the pub more often!"

That night I had attended the leaving party of one of my colleagues and, although I didn't know who would be attending, I plucked up the courage and went alone because we liked each other and I wanted to be there for him. When I arrived at the pub, which was within walking distance of the office, I was relieved to find that it was full of people I already knew, not only from my team but from other departments and even from outside the company. After having ummed and ahhed about going, I was glad to be there and did my best to integrate into the different groups who chatted cheerfully over drinks.

It's not always easy for us to know how to approach those groups of two or three people and join in their conversation. It is worth being a little daring and make the effort to do so because it opens up the opportunity for us to attend many events which are both useful and enjoyable.

On the way home on the train I began to think and suddenly I realised that as well as meeting people there who I already knew, most of them also knew each other. What surprised me was observing how people who, as far as I had known, were not connected and had no reason to interact in our company, in fact knew each other very well and had fairly close relationships. I also realised that those individuals whom I considered to be skilled at office politics stood out like beacons in the middle of the environment which made up that network of people. I saw it clearly:

> ⚠ **RELATIONSHIPS THAT ARE APPARENTLY NOT STRICTLY NECESSARY CAN BE THE KEY TO OUR SUCCESS IN ANY ORGANISATION.**

For many years I had been focusing on the quality of my work, taking care of my team and being a high performer but never realised that investing in relationships was something as necessary as it was useful.

Reflecting on this, I discovered that many of the problems and stressful situations I had faced in the workplace had something in common: my relationships with the people involved were inadequate.

> ⚠ **DON'T PUT ALL YOUR FOCUS ON YOUR IMMEDIATE SURROUNDINGS. LOOK OUTWARDS AND YOUR PERSPECTIVE WILL CHANGE.**

I felt angry with myself for having needed forty years on this planet and twenty years of professional experience to realise this. I was overwhelmed by feelings of frustration and regret for not having heard the blatant truth so clearly voiced by my experiences. Now, years later, I look back with compassion towards myself and understand that this had to be my path which has led to sharing this light of insight with you today.

Relationships are SUPER IMPORTANT (and I use capital letters on purpose) to achieve success in any organisation. We know it in our private lives, we value them and we are aware that we need to invest time and effort into them.

This principle also applies to work interactions and yet many of us don't put it on our list of priorities. Focusing on the tasks at hand is not enough to be effective and make progress in our career.

We are all at the centre of a system. A 360° environment exists around us. That environment, and navigating it properly, is a powerful tool we can use to increase our ability to influence, get the things we want, be effective in the role, and be happier.

That map in which we operate has several territories. If we are able to explore all areas within it, we will be more successful as well as enjoy higher satisfaction. If you stop to think about it, you probably know individuals who are good at taking care of one of those dimensions. We say, for example, "That person is very good at managing his boss but lousy with his team." Or the other way around. In my experience, taking care of relationships in all directions is essential to achieve the right balance in our performance. I call it working the 360° map - that is, to take care of your environment in all directions and not merely concentrate on the area that seems most important to us or where we feel comfortable.

With all the responsibilities we have and the long to-do list, we sometimes struggle to create spaces to explore our 360° map. That is why it is good to keep in mind the importance of that map and make an effort to explore it, sowing seeds in the process with the potential for them to germinate at the right time.

A good starting point is to draw our own 360° map, identifying people with power or groups with influence. Once the groups or individuals of interest have been highlighted, we must analyse the quality and quantity of our relationships with them. This small analysis makes it easier for us to identify people who may hold the keys to the goals we pursue and with whom we can improve our relationships. This can be the basis for creating an action plan and proactively cultivating those connections.

There are four types of relationship (territories on the map) that we can take care of at work:

- The network in general.
- Colleagues.
- Line managers and seniors.
- Your direct team.

> [!] CULTIVATING YOUR MAP AND YOUR REPUTATION IN ALL DIRECTIONS WILL ACHIEVE THE RESULTS WE ARE LOOKING FOR.

> [!] IF YOU BALANCE THE SCALES ACROSS ALL GROUPS YOU WILL INCREASE YOUR CHANCES OF SUCCESS.

THE NETWORK IN GENERAL

I remember my first role as team leader of more than thirty people in a multinational company within leisure and tourism. My team supported other areas across the finance department. I was full of ideas and was really determined to do a great job. I took time to understand the tasks performed by my team, making efforts to earn their respect and trust. I looked into the existing processes, searching for ideas to improve everyone's experience in delivering their job. There were opportunities for improvement everywhere and I had more good intentions and ideas than hours available.

I felt like a heroine who came from a different planet to rescue the people on my team, like Wonder Woman, unstoppable in my mission. This memory makes me smile. How naïve my intentions were! I knew it could make a positive impact on both the team members' experience and on the effectiveness of the department so I put all my efforts into carrying out many of the improvement projects I had identified.

Everything went well until, in one of the projects, I needed the heads of other departments to come onboard with the new processes that I wanted to implement. I also needed help securing elements that I didn't have at my disposal, such as data reports which my team couldn't create. Those who could assist me, of course, were not always willing to take on the extra work, which sometimes led to a sudden halt in the process.

I had been working for weeks on a new billing system so that users who were spread throughout Europe could make invoice requests. With the support of a technical consultant we developed a new online platform allowing users to make requests within a framework that would prevent billing errors, which were the norm in the existing system which generated many issues. The last step before launching the system was to show it to the chief financial officer of the travel agency division, which was the one that used it. I had prepared the meeting thoroughly, I was clear about the advantages of the new system and I was satisfied that with the new process, we would all save a lot of time. It would also help users who didn't know anything about billing technicalities to follow the process simply.

Shortly after the meeting began, I realised that this man was not listening to me. In fact, his attitude was critical towards my department in general. I had a hard time keeping the conversation focused on the billing system. He just wanted to complain that there were many overdue queries waiting to be handled by my department. As I showed him the functionality of my new system, he burst my bubbles one by one, picking faults and showing little interest.

I still remember with horror what I felt in my body. A nervous tingling was running through my temples and an intense heat in my stomach. How was it possible that they did not want to adapt to the proposed changes? Weeks of work and enthusiasm had been unexpectedly punctured like a beach ball.

With time and hindsight, I have realised that in any environment, work related or otherwise, we need to look outwards. Concentrating only on our immediate environment is not enough to achieve what we want and the goals we seek without taking into account the circumstances and needs of others, because even if they are achieved, they can still have a bitter taste.

From another perspective I realise that, in that particular situation, it took me too long to involve the leaders of those who would need to consent to the new process.

> ⚠ INVOLVING THE PEOPLE WHO WILL BE AFFECTED BY THE CHANGES WE WANT TO MAKE IN THE INITIAL PHASE OF DEFINING A PROJECT IS KEY. IT'S THE WAY TO MAKE SURE THAT WHEN THE IMPLEMENTATION PHASE COMES, THEY WILL SUPPORT THOSE CHANGES.

> ⚠ FINDING REALISTIC AND BALANCED SOLUTIONS REQUIRES A GOOD UNDERSTANDING OF THE NEEDS OF THOSE WHO WILL BE AFFECTED BY OUR PROPOSALS.

To carry out any solution successfully, the support of others is essential. Dedicating time and effort to truly listen to those around us promotes relationships that are flexible and trusting. This includes connections where the immediate goal is not obvious. The aim is to weave a network of contacts, inside and outside our organisation.

These people provide us with a great deal along our journey, such as information, without which it would be difficult for us to move forward and find solutions to the challenges that arise. With good communication, they will be understanding and receptive to our ideas, adding their contributions so that the goals we propose can become a reality. They will realise that they can count on us to listen when they identify potential opportunities and will also warn us about new risks looming on the horizon.

Little by little, our network becomes a great asset that will accompany us through different projects and jobs; a common thread woven over the years to support us when we need it.

Creating a network inside and outside your organisation is a long-distance race. Your contacts in other departments will support you to achieve what you need. The system outside your company will become important as you progress in your career - past and present colleagues, managers and advisors. Even if you don't see results straight away, building your network slowly but surely will help you find solutions, create opportunities and build your reputation.

COLLEAGUES

This group of relationships posed different challenges for me. We learn from a young age to compare ourselves with others and eventually find ourselves in the workplace, with many other intelligent and ambitious people. The shadow of fear is always present, even if we fail to acknowledge it.

In the conscious world, colleagues are a source of support, fun and collaboration, while unconsciously we may perceive them as a possible threat. Direct colleagues, without us always being aware, are able to awaken negative feelings, for instance if we think that they are more popular or skilled than we are and might get the promotion that we seek.

In my case, these invisible feelings made me build a wall of protection, collaborating and being supportive, but always on guard in case the perceived threat became a reality.

Although I see myself as a reasonable person and tend to avoid aggressive confrontations, on one occasion I had a rather fraught argument with a colleague during a meeting with our common boss. I was furious with her because I held her responsible for my having to fire a member of my team, in my view, unfairly. My boss had pressured me to fire him because of the opinion my peer had of him and his performance. I was frustrated by the circumstances. I recognised that there were aspects that prevented this person from achieving what was expected of him and I was disheartened that they didn't understand those aspects because they were outside the department. I felt attacked because my colleague's influence had carried more weight than my own in managing the situation.

This incident aroused a lot of antipathy towards this person; not on a personal level, but professionally. Now, in the cold light of day, I realise that I hadn't taken enough care of our relationship to be able to influence her opinion. My starting position was to be on the defensive.

> **WHEN WE'RE ON THE DEFENSIVE, WE DON'T ALLOW OURSELVES TO SHOW OUR VULNERABILITY, AND THAT VULNERABILITY MAY BE PRECISELY WHAT ENCOURAGES OTHERS TO HELP US.**

In addition, with the passage of time, I see that this defensive position also skewed my view of what was happening, as I was more concerned with 'protecting my tribe' than listening to criticism of this team member.

It's true that people don't always play fair and square, and that we can feel betrayed. However, from a broader perspective, I recognise that maintaining a defensive attitude put obstacles in my way and that fact slowed down some of my initiatives because I did not have enough support from my peers.

As a team leader, I sometimes felt alone. As time went by and taking carefully calculated risks, some of my close colleagues became great allies. They supported me before others and, above all, they did not undermine me in front of our line manager.

Our own intuition should enable us to distinguish colleagues who are good, trusted team players from whom to develop strategic alliances. By this, I mean people towards whom we may not feel a natural affinity but with whom we could build comfortable working relationships. It's impossible to feel totally at ease with every individual we meet along the way, as we are all different with a wide variety of personalities. Some people have styles with which we unintentionally clash. The level of depth and trust within the relationship will depend on each individual but having good links with all our direct colleagues is a great tool to develop within the company.

Within the remits of your professional ambition, you may come to perceive some of your colleagues as competitors. Although this can be true, they can also be allies. When you want to make changes, they can make the difference between you getting support from other sources or not. They can also give you the space to explore ideas and foster your sense of belonging.

One area of reflection that I find interesting is to start joining up the dots to see what kind of individuals we have struggled with in the past.

> 💬 **THE PEOPLE WE AVOID OR CLASH WITH ARE THE ONES WHO CAN TEACH US THE MOST ABOUT OURSELVES.**

📝 I will give you my advice, experiences, and everything I think can help you regarding our blind spots in chapter 12.

I came to realise that many moments of conflict in my working life had been with women similar to me. I noticed that these interactions had awakened distant childhood feelings; moments when I did not feel as valued as my classmates at school and, unconsciously, those memories had become the barrier to that type of relationship at work. The mere fact of realising this was the first step to not allowing myself to get carried away by those unconscious tendencies, to take a step back and assess the situation objectively and to behave more mindfully.

LINE MANAGERS AND SENIORS

This group is the one that arouses the most mixed feelings; from admiration and gratitude to frustration and insecurity. The quality of interactions and situations with those to whom we report have had, and will continue to have, a great impact on our work experience. Our ability to manage this type of bond is what determines, to a large extent, the life story we perceive and also the experience of those in the work environment who report to us directly. Let's therefore approach this relationship with great respect in both directions.

In our relationships with some bosses, everything goes smoothly: they make demands on us, support us and also teach us. Others give rise to feelings of uneasiness, discomfort and uncertainty.

If it has been harder for you to connect with some, but not others, ask yourself: what do those who made it difficult have in common? Behind those characteristics you will find the patterns that lead to your feelings of unease. Observe them and become aware that while these individuals were all different, your behaviour towards each of them was different too. You will, hopefully, reach the conclusion that you are, in part, responsible for such outcomes.

> 🛈 SOMETIMES IT'S EASIER FOR US TO PUT ALL THE BLAME ON OUR SENIORS WITHOUT LOOKING IN THE MIRROR AND ADMITTING THAT WE CONTRIBUTE TO WHAT HAPPENS.

During my first year in a multinational media company, I had three bosses in succession, each with a different personal style, with different priorities and on their own learning curve. Adapting to a new manager is hard, but it is also an opportunity if we manage the situation intelligently. When a new line manager arrives, we have the opportunity to prove our worth, as this person has not yet acquired the internal know-how about the company or the department. Becoming the provider of the 'organisational intelligence', which they need, gives us the opportunity to build a relationship. By highlighting the capabilities that we possess within our areas of responsibility, we can become someone they trust.

With the first boss in this job, I made the mistake of letting her set the rhythm of the relationship. She was overwhelmed and already had her own circle of trusted colleagues, so she didn't devote any of her time to me. I had started this role feeling out of my comfort zone, her personal style intimidated me and I pulled back and started doing what I thought was necessary on my own. This proved to be a big mistake, because I took steps forward without keeping her sufficiently informed and without taking into account the expectations she had.

There were days when, as I left the office, my tears would be falling throughout my twenty-minute walk to the train station. A grown woman, with a solid professional track record, was feeling like a little girl who has just been told off at school. My entire body tense and my eyes puffy and red, I felt totally lost and unable to share my emotional state with anyone, neither at home nor with my peers. During that period, I felt inferior and believed that the one who was out of place was me.

We tend to think that superiors simply are the way they are and we have to accept them. To some extent that is true, although it is possible to be proactive in managing the relationship to enrich the experience. If your boss doesn't create spaces for you to talk privately, ask for them. If they don't set clear objectives or instructions, make the proposal yourself and discuss them together. If there's something that worries or bothers you, find a way to express it non-confrontationally. If you need help, ask for it. If you want to say no, do so.

In my case, I have had line managers with aggressive leadership styles who didn't take me seriously enough. They followed their habitual pace until I was the one who changed the dynamics, sharing the reins of the relationship. In this way I began to influence their expectations and achieved their respect.

I will show you some tricks that can empower you in the relationship with your boss in chapter 4.

These connections need trust and good communication, even if it's hard to find the opportunities or courage to do so.

> ⚠️ **IF YOUR MANAGER IS NOT PROACTIVE IN ENSURING THAT YOUR NEEDS ARE BEING MET, YOU CAN TAKE THE INITIATIVE.**

This way, you will gain influence over your workload and environment, get support and grow by learning.

In this group it is also convenient to take into account those senior to whom you report. It is essential to make an effort to build bonds with people higher up in the organisation. They will also have a say in initiatives you want to promote and their opinion of you will influence their actions. Don't rely entirely on earning the approval of your direct superiors, you also need the approval of their peers.

In my case, the boss of the three line-managers I mentioned in the earlier example gave me advice and support during the turbulent times that the company was going through and thus became one of my great allies in the organisation. I am aware that it can be problematic finding opportunities to strengthen ties with superiors, but that is no excuse for not even trying.

You will discover the impact allies can make in chapter 3.

YOUR DIRECT TEAM

Even if we are not directly responsible for a team, we can all find opportunities to lead. The relationship with our direct team is undoubtedly marked by the personality and beliefs that we have about the role that a boss should play. The line manager or supervisor that we become is a mixture of the values and leadership styles that we have experienced professionally. We learn from our bosses, both in what we emulate and in what we avoid. That's helpful, but it's also vital to be yourself: we are all unique in our own ways.

[!] **THE BEST WAY TO LEAD YOUR TEAM IS TO BE TRUE TO YOUR OWN VALUES.**

Thus, our tone of command is easy to interpret because we set the tone for behavior and values of the group coherently. For example, respect for others is one of my values, hence I never raised my voice with my team. Your own values will be different to mine, but acknowledging them and being faithful to those principles when we are leading others strengthens our authenticity.

It is impossible to be perfect leaders. As a manager, I have made mistakes and my actions have not always been easily accepted by all my colleagues.

[!] **WHEN WE ARE HONEST WITH OUR TEAM THEY WILL SENSE IT AND, EVEN IF THEY DON'T ALWAYS AGREE, THAT SINCERITY GENERATES THE NECESSARY TRUST FOR THEM TO ROW IN THE DESIRED DIRECTION.**

At times, my behavior with my team members has been similar to the way I behave with my children. I have wanted the best for them and I have tried to guide them as best I could. At other times I would let myself get carried away by the whirlwind of work, missing good times along the way.

In my case, my approach to leading a team has often been described as atypical and, although it was challenging at times, managing people has given me a great deal of satisfaction.

Of the four territories on the 360° map, this was always the group I felt most comfortable with and where I put a large part of my effort. Of course, I also had some perplexing moments; for example, feeling intimidated by their talent at times when my self-esteem was low but this can also happen with people from other groups.

41

We are all different and you may feel like a fish out of water in one of the groups, but not as much so in the others.

Progression in our professional careers adds complexities and also increases the number of participants on our map of relationships. Our list of priorities grows relentlessly and while our free time decreases. Immersing ourselves in work and reducing our attention to the team is a temptation, especially if everything is going smoothly and, apparently, as planned. Individual contact with as many people as possible is a good investment. Find out who your team members are outside of their roles. We all like to be noticed and when a team leader makes this effort it generates loyalty, productivity and job satisfaction. Taking care of our employees will not only bring advantages to the work we do, but it is a healthy and rewarding contribution to the world in which we want to live.

Their testimony is key to whether we are doing it right. As with everything, there are individuals to whom we are more attuned than others. Ask yourself:

- Do the people in my team trust me?
- Do they come to me when they have a problem to solve?
- Do they freely express their opinions when they disagree with me?

When your position involves being responsible for others, the team is the asset we have to enable us to achieve personal and departmental goals. Our management of these people impacts our performance and job satisfaction. Each team is different, with different cultures, trajectories and circumstances. That is why we need to adapt the strategy we choose when we acquire responsibility for a new team.

> In chapter 3 I will tell you about a strategy that I have found almost infallible whenever I have had to seek consensus.

In one of my roles, my team was well-established and had been working together with few changes in personnel for many years. The level of maturity of many finance processes was quite low. Instead of charging in like a bull in a china-shop and making sweeping changes, I got them involved in jointly defining our situation and needs, thus identifying common problems and areas of potential development. This work made the speed of change somewhat slow at first but, once the working group had assimilated what we could achieve, it was much easier to carry out the changes we conceived together.

It took me years to learn that solutions developed as a team have firmer roots than those that we define alone. Without the contribution of these associates, we only consider our own agenda, wasting the vision that they are able to contribute.

Taking time to identify the feelings and needs of others is also a vital step towards earning their trust and being able to make profound changes together.

My experience has led me to the following conclusion:

TO HAVE REAL INFLUENCE IN ORGANISATIONS IT IS NECESSARY TO TAKE CARE OF RELATIONSHIPS AT ALL LEVELS.

Investing time and effort in cultivating bonds within our professional environment pays off in many different ways. Each type of stakeholder has a role to play. The quality of our relationships in all areas and the balance between them is a great asset in making progress and succeeding.

There are many ways to nurture those interactions. Leaving our mark on others is easier than we think. It does not always require a lot of effort or a lot of time. All we need do is pay attention and think creatively.

I am sure that if you think about it, you can remember small gestures that others have made towards you that have had a big impact, sometimes positively and sometimes with devastating effects.

Words of support, recognition or interest in something important in the lives of others are small gestures that, while not strictly necessary, are pleasant to receive and will strengthen relationships. We only have to listen and pay attention to find a thousand and one ways to pay small compliments with words that can brighten the day of those around us. It is the simplest way to cultivate a positive environment and create a culture that recognises people as individuals.

I can't tell you what amount of time is optimal to invest in your relationships; that is up to you. The ways to do it are endless, making room in your diary for individual meetings, coffees, lunches, business events and so on. Invest in these four areas and see the results. In my case, it had a massive impact!

Draw your own 360° Map. You can do this exercise in relation to your environment in general or around a given project:

- Think about the wider network in other departments or organisations, peers, seniors and your direct team.
- Make a list of five people in your environment in each of these groups.
- Identify the individuals on your list belonging to circles with power.

360 MAP OF RELATIONSHIPS

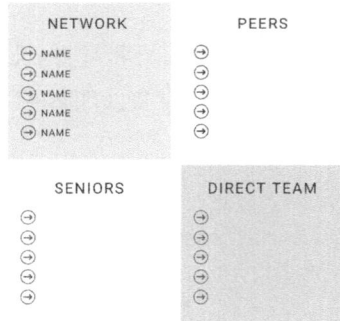

NETWORK	PEERS
→ NAME	→
→ NAME	→
→ NAME	→
→ NAME	→
→ NAME	→

SENIORS	DIRECT TEAM
→	→
→	→
→	→
→	→
→	→

360 MAP OF RELATIONSHIPS

QUALITY OF RELATIONSHIP

MAINTAIN

→ NAME
→ NAME
→ NAME
→ NAME
→ NAME

MAINTAIN

→
→
→
→
→

WATCH

→
→
→
→
→

CULTIVATE

→
→
→
→
→

LEVEL OF INFLUENCE

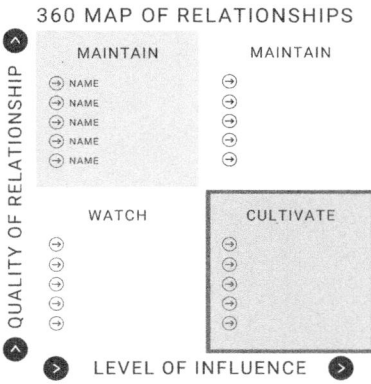

- Reflect on your relationship with them and reorganise the list according to the quality of the existing relationship and the level of influence they have.
- You will identify people who could hold the key to your objectives, with whom the relationships can be improved.
- Finally, create your own action plan to cultivate those bonds with people of influence.
- Write down what you have become aware of by carrying out this exercise.

Chapter 2
CONFLICT IS INEVITABLE

Unresolved conflicts weigh like stones in a backpack. This chapter will reveal how you can stop carrying so much weight on your back, which will nourish your personal relationships and protect your motivation.

No matter how well we try to take care of our relationships, conflict is inevitable. Your ability to manage it is key if you want to not only advance professionally but also feel comfortable in your work environment.

I remember an occasion when we spent the whole morning delivering a presentation to some investors who had come from the USA. After almost two weeks of preparation, it seemed that the session had gone smoothly and, as is customary in these cases, we all went to lunch together. Present were the rest of the management team, which included my two line-managers and the investors, all of whom were men.

Although generally I function comfortably in social situations, I must admit that these informal gatherings, where I am the only woman, make me feel like a fish out of water. They have a great time and talk about many subjects that don't interest me at all, such as cars, football and golf, amongst others. I

- as I imagine many other women do in similar situations - feel pressured to join in the conversation and try to make it look as if I fit in with everyone else. One strategy I used to use was to tell anecdotes I had heard my husband tell, making an effort to participate in the conversation.

Suddenly, my boss, laughing with one of the investors, said, "Well, we have another one," pointing at me. In an instant, my eyes widened like saucers as I stared at him with a forced smile. He was referring to the fact that there were only two women on the board. A wave of heated frustration swept through me, spoiling the rest of the lunch and unsettling me. I was furious! My level of commitment and respect for him changed from ten to zero in a matter of seconds.

I kept thinking about it all weekend and brooding over the incident was just adding fuel to the fire, feeding my feelings of antagonism towards him. "He doesn't take me seriously." "He believes that, because I am a woman, I am less worthy than my peers, who are always applauding his peacock displays." "He thinks that because I have a sympathetic leadership style, I am weak." "I'm sick of him not valuing me or taking me seriously." "I'm going to start looking for another job immediately!" The list of negative phrases was repeated endlessly in my thoughts, like a scratched record, turning what was just a few seconds of a conversation into something that had had a harmful effect on both my emotional state and my desire to face work on Monday morning.

In chapter 14 I will tell you my strategies for making peace with your self-talk.

Conflict takes many different forms; words that hurt us, foolish arguments or circumstances where our needs and those of others collide.

Conflicts are a reality in all the areas we operate in: family, personal and work relationships.

When we least expect it, conflict appears like a slap in the face, leaving us perplexed and creating a wave of emotion which drags us down into an ocean of negative feelings.

Despite being an everyday occurrence, we are rarely taught how to resolve conflicts. We learn through trial and error over the years and many people never manage it. Some of us do our best to avoid conflict situations: we pretend that nothing has happened and that the problem does not exist, like the proverbial ostrich. Unfortunately, without our even realising it, the original conflict then grows like an avalanche until it crushes us without warning.

Each person reacts to conflict in their own way. As I mentioned, many people avoid it whilst others face it full on, like a bullfighter, and others confront it but without any real attempt to seek resolution. There are also those who find it impossible to make themselves heard, even if they try to stand up to a conflict. There are as many ways to deal with conflict as there are people on earth, but you may have found that you can identify with one of the styles of response I just described.

In the organisations where I have worked, I have had the opportunity to witness how people who were very capable in their own right could not collaborate well with some colleagues, often because they had not resolved conflicts or had dealt with them badly. Over time, these unresolved conflicts became major walls and had a negative impact on their ability to work alongside others and their level of satisfaction at work.

Let's go back to that incident with my boss which disturbed me so much. The damage he caused hadn't really been just because of his comment. That was the straw that broke the camel's back after many previous situations which had fed on my personal insecurities. All those things I had said to myself at the time came from beliefs and doubts which I had accumulated during the time we had worked together, and all of it because we had communication barriers and unresolved issues.

> 💬 IT IS POSSIBLE TO FEEL OFFENDED NOT ONLY BY A SPECIFIC INCIDENT, BUT BY THE ACCUMULATION OF SMALL UNRESOLVED FRICTIONS THAT GET TO A POINT WHERE THEY BECOME UNBEARABLE.

My frustration was massive and I just wanted to confront him, even though I was well aware that it could have serious consequences and affect both our relationship and my job stability.

I realised that the damage was done and that doing nothing about it would only distance us further and diminish my enjoyment of many aspects of my role. Since I had been thinking about changing jobs anyway, I concluded that I had nothing to lose by trying, at the very least, to vent my frustrations by letting him know how I felt. I also knew that it was sensible to choose my words carefully and attempt to air my feelings without provoking a defensive response from him.

> **CONFLICTS DON'T TEND TO GO AWAY ON THEIR OWN. THEY CAN SNOWBALL UNTIL IT'S TOO LATE TO RESOLVE THEM.**

So, as they say, let's take the bull by the horns and resolve conflicts proactively before they hurt us at a time when we least expect it.

This does not mean that we have to get stuck in without preparation and in the heat of the moment - far from it. Good conflict management can become almost an art. It requires willingness, patience, practice and continuous learning.

Over the years, I have developed my own personal method of managing conflicts and although it is not infallible, it has served me well on many occasions. This method is useful regardless of your style, whether you are one of those who throw themselves into the fray in the heat of the moment, those who flee or those who stay in the middle. These steps will help balance your natural style and achieve better results. If it's useful to you, great, and if not, I encourage you to think about your own experiences and define your own personal method.

This method will support you in resolving conflicts in four steps:

- Previous precautions.
- Basic premise.

- Plan.
- Be prepared to listen.

PREVIOUS PRECAUTIONS

During moments of conflict our nerves are usually on the surface. It is essential to take some precautions so that the succession of events does not get out of hand.

Never respond to a difficult interaction in the heat of the moment. When conflict catches us by surprise and we have not had the opportunity to think, the worst thing we can do is react impulsively. It is better to pause, not respond immediately and, if necessary, ask the person involved to give us time before we respond.

MANY OCCASIONS THAT LEAD TO REGRET ARE THOSE WHEN WE HAVE BEEN CARRIED AWAY BY EMOTION.

Responding to conflicts immediately only exacerbates them.

I remember a meeting when my line-manager made me a proposal for changes to my role that I was not keen to accept. Furthermore, his way to approach me was quite aggressive and did not sit well with me at all. Instead of telling him at the time what I thought, I said, "I understand the reasons for your proposal. It's something I didn't expect, so let me think about it and we'll meet at another time to discuss it. I don't want to be rushed into it without having considered all the implications." He, of course, would have liked to settle the matter there and then but, by my asking for time politely, he was left with no choice but to smile reluctantly and end the conversation. Then I thought, "Good thing I bit my lip!"

> [!] WHEN SOMETHING CATCHES US BY SURPRISE THERE ARE USUALLY FUNDAMENTAL CONSIDERATIONS TO KEEP IN MIND WHICH, AT THAT INSTANT, DO NOT COME TO MIND.

> [!] HAVING TIME TO THINK WITHOUT PRESSURE IS IMPORTANT, NOT ONLY TO MANAGE CONFLICT, BUT TO MAKE SURE THAT WE DON'T LOSE POWER IN NEGOTIATION SITUATIONS.

BASIC PREMISE

Human beings do not usually wake up in the morning seeking to enter into conflicts with others. We tend to fall into them accidentally, so remembering this fact allows us to take a step back from the scene and try not to take conflict personally.

I raise my hand and confess that this is difficult to put into practice. Not taking situations personally is a big challenge. Despite this, it is worth continuing to try again and again, even if, from time to time, we fail. In the aforementioned lunch meeting, I was taking what my boss said totally and absolutely personally, thinking that I had reason to be offended and that he was a brute without an ounce of emotional intelligence. *Mea culpa!* This is a key part of the conflict resolution process and we all have a hard time recognising it without making a conscious effort. The conversation I later had with my boss made me realise this clearly.

There is much written about how we interpret each situation in relation to our realities, past experiences, values and beliefs.

> [!] OUR PERCEPTION OF THE WORLD IS NEVER THE SAME AS THAT OF OTHERS.

Things are neither black nor white; they depend on the interpretation of each one.

I'll tell you why it will be helpful for you to recognise this in chapter 10.

WHEN WE GET ANGRY WITH OTHERS, NO MATTER HOW ANNOYING OR OFFENSIVE THE SITUATION MAY SEEM TO US, THEY ARE LIVING IT FROM THEIR POINT OF VIEW, WHICH IS NOT THE SAME AS OUR OWN.

Realising this helps to dissociate ourselves a little from what is happening and see it in a more objective way.

A good trick is to think about what needs the other person is trying to satisfy by pursuing their position. Although it may be difficult for us to identify them, they are always there and trying to recognise them, even without understanding them, is a good starting point towards a resolution of the conflict.

PLAN

Once calm, we are more prepared to evaluate what has happened more objectively. This is useful, if only to analyse the circumstances.

SORTING OUT OUR IDEAS IS A GOOD WAY TO HELP US PLAN THE CONVERSATION WITH THE PERSON OR PEOPLE INVOLVED, AT THE RIGHT TIME.

For me, writing down my thoughts is the best way to organise my ideas. I've been preparing difficult meetings for years, armed with my notebook of key points carefully crafted before I start the conversation. The incident of my meltdown over my boss's unfortunate comment was no exception: I created my list carefully before attending the meeting I had requested to address the situation.

It is not always easy to digest our experiences and identify which are our most basic needs in order to seek them.

> **IT IS USEFUL TO ASK YOURSELF SOME QUESTIONS TO GET TO THE BOTTOM OF THE MATTER AND ALSO LEAVE ASIDE ASPECTS THAT, ALTHOUGH PRESENT, ARE NOT REALLY IMPORTANT.**

Let's say that the intention of this exercise is to find the main points of a possible conversation or negotiation.

- What emotions has the conflict aroused in me?
- Has the other person realised that, for me, this is a problem?
- What would be the consequences if I don't do anything about it?
- If I could ask for help without any anxiety, what would I ask of them?
- Why do I need these things?
- What alternatives are there?
- What does this individual have to gain by supporting me?
- What am I asking for which has given rise to this conflictive situation?
- How can I assist him or her?
- What would be the possible implications if I face the situation and this person reacts badly?
- If it goes well, what would I achieve?
- What aspects of my behavior in the past have created conflict from their perspective?
- What do they need that I have been unable, or not wanted, to give them?

The list could be endless but I hope that these examples will widen your view of the situation to a more global perspective and not yours alone.

These types of questions provide us with the keys to finding solutions which, after all, is what we are trying to achieve. Find a path towards your mutual benefit or, at least, one where the situation does not become a ticking timebomb for the relationship in the future.

This reflection will facilitate the answer to three fundamental questions:

- What do I need from that person to resolve the conflict?
- How can I help them in a way which results in the issue also being resolved from their perspective?
- What are the key messages I need to convey about the situation?

With these three clear ideas you have the necessary tools to have a conversation, which should always be face to face – in person or by videoconference, if the former is not possible.

> ⚠ IN CONFLICT RESOLUTION SITUATIONS, THE OPPORTUNITY TO LOOK AT EACH OTHER, LISTEN AND REACT ACCORDINGLY IS FUNDAMENTAL.

Never convey these messages in writing, as as this can be like placing all your chips on a single slot on a roulette wheel. When we deal with sensitive topics in writing we miss the opportunity to tweak our perspective or adapt the words we use, considering the other person's reaction.

> ⚠ DO NOT MISS THE OPPORTUNITY TO USE ALL OF THE COMMUNICATION TOOLS WE HAVE, SUCH AS TONE OF VOICE, VOLUME AND BODY LANGUAGE.

It is said that, in emotionally charged situations, only 7% of communication depends on the words we use.

The next step is to approach the conversation. Being in a calm, less emotional state and with clear ideas, it will be much easier to find an agreement.

It is advisable to let the person you want to talk to know that you would like to have a conversation about the specific topic in order to find a common solution.

Avoid surprises. In my experience, when people are surprised they may react defensively, so there is a chance that the situation will worsen.

When you ask this person for time to deal with the issue, try to convey cordiality and encouragement to seek solutions rather than complaints or reproaches. In that way, they can also think about it and prepare if they wish.

BE PREPARED TO LISTEN

Place and time are also decisive. If possible, choose a neutral place and over a coffee. Look for an environment that offers you some privacy and ensure that you have enough time to finish the conversation.

If you have no choice but to have a meeting in the office, try to sit next to each other and not in a way that incites a sense of opposition. Don't be afraid to have your notebook handy so you can make sure you follow your key messages plan as it demonstrates professionalism and preparation.

Our choice of words is paramount. It always helps to make positive affirmations instead of negative ones. Also, do not to refer to what the other person has done, but to how we feel about it. Instead of saying, "You don't value me," or, "You don't make enough time for us to meet in person," we can say, "That comment made me feel unvalued," or, "I would benefit a lot if we had a weekly meeting to look at outstanding issues." Words are not neutral and have different connotations for each person. For example, the word 'soft' might imply tenderness for some people but weakness for others. Similarly, it's better to use the word 'situation' instead of 'problem'.

> ⚠ PAYING ATTENTION TO THE WORDS WE USE MAKES IT EASIER TO HAVE LESS EMOTIONALLY CHARGED CONVERSATIONS BY CONSCIOUSLY CHOOSING LESS AGGRESSIVE OPTIONS.

During the meeting, take the initiative and set out the context. Tell the other person that you are aware that the circumstance, or incident, has created a conflict between you and that your goal for the conversation is to have a dialogue about your mutual needs and find a solution that will help you both.

You can present a summary of the situation and explain why that creates a conflict for you.

> ⚠ MAKE SURE THAT IN YOUR PRESENTATION YOU SHOW THEM THAT YOU HAVE ALSO DONE YOUR BEST TO VIEW WHAT HAPPENED FROM THEIR PERSPECTIVE.

> ⚠ INVITE HIM OR HER TO ADD ANY ASPECTS THAT YOU HAVE NOT IDENTIFIED BUT WHICH ARE IMPORTANT TO THEM.

If the person opens up to the conversation and you listen actively, your interpretation of the situation will be likely to change as you will receive new information or clear up any confusion. In my experience, many of the conflicts that occur in the workplace are the result of misunderstandings rather than differences that are truly significant.

During the conversation you will be able to agree on mutual solutions based on your mutual needs once you have considered all the information that, without a doubt, you were lacking before having that exchange.

An important element is knowing how to choose not only the messages we want to convey but also at what point to let them flow as part of the conversation.

> ⚠ IT IS NOT A QUESTION OF RECITING A LIST OF DEMANDS, BUT OF ALLOWING YOURSELF TO BE CARRIED ALONG BY THE CONVERSATION AND WAITING FOR THE OPPORTUNE MOMENT TO DELIVER ALL THE KEY POINTS.

Even if we do not manage to deliver every single one of them, simply making many of those points and having that conversation generates a lot of goodwill.

The person's reaction is out of our hands. Despite that, if we have a proactive and collaborative attitude, the chances of resolution are greater than if we do nothing. So the next time you find yourself in a conflict with someone with whom you're going to continue working in the future, I encourage you do your best to manage it with your own initiative.

In the event that the conversation does not go according to plan, you will have done everything in your power, with the best possible intentions. This collaborative behavior will help cement your reputation as someone looking for solutions rather than putting barriers in the way of others.

You may be wondering how the meeting with my boss went. Happily, it went very well and we reached a resolution not only because it cleared the air but because I learned a great deal in the process, specifically that I had not put myself in their position or taken a step back to contextualise. In fact, when I explained how I felt, the same conversation led me to realise that although he sometimes said phrases that shocked me, many of the negative aspects which I had perceived had been generated by my own insecurities. I was, nevertheless, still unable on that occasion to apply this method one hundred percent but despite this, addressing the conflict voluntarily contributed to mitigating the clash and opening up new paths of understanding and work collaboration, without the weight of unresolved issues in the background.

Think about a conflict situation you've faced recently:

- Briefly summarise what happened.
- Review the previous sentence and evaluate if it is objective or if there are aspects you have overlooked. Correct the summary if necessary.
- Identify three key ideas that you would like, or would have liked, to convey in order to vent your frustrations.
- Describe what you would like to see happen to resolve this conflict.
- Considering the method covered in this chapter, write down what you could have done differently to alleviate or resolve the conflict.
- Identify what you can still do to resolve or mitigate the conflict.
- Write down what you have become aware of by doing this exercise.

Chapter 3

OTHERS CAN BE OF GREAT HELP

Most of us have a tendency to believe that we should be able to deal with everything on our own. The reasons are many, from arrogance or lack of confidence, to the belief that others do not want to, or cannot, help. Leaving those useless motivations behind helps us to move forward and collaborate in ways we couldn't even imagine.

The reality is that, as we saw in chapter 1, we live in an established system and therefore others do have a role to play. It's up to us to push the balance to the point where others provide us with support, rather than opposition.

In this chapter we will explore four aspects that will give you resources to receive assistance from others:

- Building a consensus makes everything easier.
- Shared decisions.
- Asking for help works.
- Mentors and allies.

BUILDING A CONSENSUS MAKES EVERYTHING EASIER

In our work environment, we often spend hours preparing Power Point presentations or reports; the purpose being to persuade someone to accept what we propose, often during the course of an important meeting. That someone could be our line manager, the entire team or part of it, another department, or a client.

We prepare the proposals with care, trying to provide those who are going to receive them with good reasons to concur. We try to make the data presented clearly structured, and offer compelling arguments. Finally, our big day arrives, with some nerves, and we are confident that we have all the facts needed to persuade our audience. The meeting begins and everything goes smoothly ... at first! The attendees listen and suddenly someone asks a question or makes a comment that derails the entire presentation.

I recall some of these meetings perfectly. For one of these, I had power-dressed for the occasion, determined to be unfazed by doubts or objections that anyone might express; fully prepared to defend any question or pushback. When someone then flung a totally unexpected question at me, I immediately noticed that the atmosphere of the meeting had changed and I felt like I'd been thrown into the lion's den. I tried to say that the answer to that question would be explained later in the presentation but I felt flustered and panicked, as the energy with which I had entered the room seemed to drain away through my feet, leaving me shaking and unsteady. What a disappointment! On more than one occasion, I was not even able to finish the entire proposal, despite having spent so many hours preparing for the meeting. I felt so frustrated and dissatisfied!

I remember one day, I was flabbergasted at the monthly board meeting. My colleague, the marketing director, had just finished presenting his monthly slot. I imagine that if anyone had noticed my face, they would have seen my raised eyebrows and bewildered face. He had made a rather bold proposal to increase the size of his team and the investment in the marketing budget. In a matter of minutes, before I had had time to process this, everything was agreed and authorised. Our CEO had not even asked for my opinion. At that moment I saw it clearly: the outcome of the meeting was already cut and dried.

> ⚠ **IMPORTANT MEETINGS ARE SOMETIMES A FORMALITY; TOPICS ARE DISCUSSED AND AGREED INFORMALLY BEFORE THE MEETING BEGINS.**

It may seem obvious to some, but it took me quite a while to realise this. However, once the message landed, it had a big impact on my behavior and my ability to pull off initiatives that went beyond my department or direct control.

The vast majority of the initiatives we want to carry out in the workplace need the cooperation or authorization of other people, so this is, in my opinion, part of the key to success.

> ⚠ **TO BRING THE PROPOSALS WE WANT TO FRUITION, IT HELPS A GREAT DEAL TO CARRY OUT DIPLOMATIC WORK PRIOR TO THE MEETINGS WHERE, IN THEORY, YOU MUST INITIALLY PRESENT THESE PROPOSALS.**

Some people can do this instinctively. They are the ones who we perceive as being good at office politics. The rest of us can learn!

In my first position as CFO, I felt that it was important to change the reporting mechanisms which the organisation had been using for years. The information presented at the board meetings was not very practical as it contained too much detail. Each department presented its own KPIs (Key Performance Indicators) but nothing was mentioned that would link them all together into global metrics to measure our joint responsibility as a management team. I had several obstacles ahead if I wanted to carry out these changes; two of them being particularly tricky.

The first was that the CEO had been using the same information for many years and it was he who had created the current method used. As the person responsible for finance, I had the knowledge and experience to define what was appropriate. However, the CEO liked the existing way of reporting and he was reluctant to share too much information with the rest of the management team. He seemed to believe that holding some information back gave him superpowers, leaving him the only person with the ability to have overall vision - as if sharing information would weaken him as Kryptonite did to Superman!

Secondly, the culture of the organisation was uncollaborative and the idea of having KPIs to measure performance in departments generated fear and discomfort. There were no shared aspirations across departments. It was not uncommon for decisions at department level to benefit their own indicators while creating negative consequences for other parts of the organisation.

Many people, including members of my team, warned me that I would find it difficult, if not impossible, to persuade the CEO to accept the change I wanted. I prepared a presentation, as visual as possible, with a monthly reporting proposal which included new KPIs and some common targets for everyone. For several weeks I held meetings with the heads of the most important departments. I listened to their opinions, not only about my proposal, but about what frustrated them about the current method. Although this work was laborious, it ultimately paid off. One could compare it to preparing a really complicated recipe: when it's served and on the table, we're glad it's over, but we can't help feeling proud.

A possible method to build consensus without exhausting ourselves in the process has four steps:

- Identifying key people.
- Holding one-on-one meetings.
- Adapting our proposal.
- Presenting the proposal and effecting wider communication.

IDENTIFYING KEY PEOPLE

Key people are those who have the power to decide, their confidants, and people who you assess will be against or in favor. Identify people who meet these requirements regarding the subject matter you're working on. There can be many proposals that need consensus: process changes, projects with a need for a budget, new hires in your team, and many others.

When you are clear about which people have the ability to support or slow down your mission, you will find it easier to start work on building consensus for your proposal.

> ⚠️ IT IS NOT ABOUT CARRYING OUT AN ELECTORAL CAMPAIGN, BUT ABOUT INVESTING TIME AND EFFORT IN ENSURING THAT KEY PEOPLE HAVE THE OPPORTUNITY TO FEEL INVOLVED, AS WELL AS AVOIDING SURPRISES.

Giving unexpected information out of the blue can generate resistance, so the less frequently we do it, the better - especially in public.

We all like to feel important and be heard, so when we approach someone and tell them that we are working on some ideas and that we would appreciate their perspective and contribution, they are very likely to want to cooperate.

HOLDING ONE-ON-ONE MEETINGS

Once you've identified influencers, you can start having one-on-one conversations with each of them. The format and duration of these sessions may vary depending on the level of influence of the person and the relationship you have with them. It can be done during an informal conversation over coffee or even going through the draft of your Power Point presentation or project document together and going into more detail.

Always present your proposal as a draft, subject to changes that can improve it once their perspective is considered.

> ⚠ I RECOMMEND THAT YOU LEAVE THE MOST IMPORTANT OR DIFFICULT PERSON UNTIL THE END, SO YOU CAN INTEGRATE INTO THE FINAL CONVERSATION WHAT YOU HAVE LEARNED DURING THE PROCESS.

This will help to jump the last hurdle of this obstacle course.

ADAPT YOUR PROPOSAL

This step serves two functions. First of all, it's a strategy towards getting others to accept your ideas. Secondly, the perspectives or ideas you will gain could be very useful. With this information you can improve your proposal or identify obstacles along the way. It is better to successfully carry out a realistic initiative than to fail with a proposal that is overly utopian or impractical.

During my consensus-building process for the changes I wanted to make to the way we reported, I received many suggestions and a lot of useful information. The contributions of my colleagues assisted in improving my proposal and finding new arguments to persuade the CEO to accept it.

Being clear about the most important objectives of your proposal will help maintain consistency in your initial aspirations. You can draft an explicit list of objectives in your presentation or simply remind yourself regularly of your goals in order to safeguard them.

> ⚠ ADAPTING TO THE ENVIRONMENT AND THE NEEDS OF OTHERS IS IMPORTANT.

[!] **WE MUST TAKE CARE THAT, IN ADAPTING THEM, THE IMPORTANT COMPONENTS OF THE INITIATIVE ARE NOT LOST.**

This balance is not easy to achieve and every situation is different. If we close ourselves too much to change, we may end up carrying out initiatives which generate too much friction for the organisation - or even ones which fail before starting. On the other hand, if we are too flexible, we can implement something that is not optimal or ambitious enough. I recommend that you let yourself be guided by your intuition, leaving aside the ego that can often betray us so much.

Before making changes, ask yourself:

- How does this suggestion affect my goal list?

This will show if your possible resistance is unjustified or if, on the contrary, accepting that suggestion will damage the integrity of your initial purpose.

PRESENTING THE PROPOSAL AND EFFECTING WIDER COMMUNICATION

Once the proposal is adapted, with a good balance between your goals and the needs and opinions of others, you can start your presentation with confidence.

The final meeting, in addition to being a formality, also provides an opportunity to inform others who will be affected by the proposal, or simply need to be aware.

Those who have not participated in the consensus process may express doubts or resistance but, with the support of others, you will be more likely to be able to appease them. Don't forget to continue the communication work beyond the meeting.

⚠ MUCH OF THE RESISTANCE TO NEW INITIATIVES CAN BE ALLEVIATED WITH GOOD COMMUNICATION.

⚠ ALTHOUGH THERE WILL BE PEOPLE WHO DO NOT HAVE THE POWER TO REJECT THE PROPOSAL, THEY MAY HAVE THE INFLUENCE TO PROVIDE SUGGESTIONS AND MAKE THE IMPLEMENTATION RUN MORE SMOOTHLY.

The aforementioned steps are instinctively taken by people who we perceive to be political savvies. This ability is often frowned upon and arouses criticism from colleagues for their being the last to get to work every morning but the first to get the rewards. Does that sound familiar?

In my opinion, having put this method into practice and taking into account the advantages it brings, it is worth doing. It is an indispensable strategy for any professional who wants to have an impact on their organisation. If, in the past, you have not done this naturally, it is possible to learn. Go for it!

Think about a change you'd like to promote in your workplace or personal environment:

- Summarise your proposal in a simple sentence or paragraph.
- Make a list of all the people who have the ability to influence the outcome.
- Divide the list into two - those who you think will support your proposal and those who will potentially oppose it.
- Identify those in the list above who are particularly relevant if you want to build a consensus.
- Write down what you've noticed through doing this exercise, or by recalling a recent goal where you haven't received enough support.

SHARED DECISIONS

Sharing some decision-making with your team can be a great strategy.

We become leaders for many reasons. One of them is because of our ability to make decisions and take risks. Decision-making is key to being able to perform in positions of responsibility and achieve what we propose. Leaders frequently speak of feeling lonely — but that loneliness is part of the game.

However, this does not mean that on certain occasions it is not appropriate or intelligent, to share decision-making. It is about others also having skin in the game. You're probably wondering what I'm talking about, so let me explain. When we have a concrete interest or involvement in something, our perspectives and behaviors are radically different from when we do not.

> WHEN WE HAVE TO MAKE POTENTIALLY CONTROVERSIAL DECISIONS, DURING THE MAKING OF THOSE DECISIONS IT CAN BE USEFUL TO INVOLVE PEOPLE WHO HAVE THE POTENTIAL TO BECOME DETRACTORS DURING THE IMPLEMENTATION.

During my time as CFO in a retail company, the Finance Director (FD), who reported directly to me, decided to leave the company after many years. As the team members each had, on average, over ten years' experience within the company, it was going to be challenging to find a candidate who would be readily accepted by them. The departing FD was going to be a hard act to follow, having been respected and appreciated by everyone.

Choosing a leader comes with a great deal of responsibility. When filling a vacancy, it is always important to choose a candidate who has the right skills, experience and personality but is also a cultural fit. We all accept that it is important that the person fits into the position and that the position is also suitable for the applicant.

When it comes to selecting someone to lead a team, there are other subtleties beyond those commonly held considerations. Especially in cases where there are other people who will be affected by our choice, it is important that we go further than that, thinking three-dimensionally, rather than just in two dimensions. The candidate's success depends not only on their fit into the position, but within their team, especially with the people who will report to that person directly.

The selection process provides a great opportunity for the future leader of a team to take their first steps to building the relationships with their future team and also to make sure that their subordinates want to see them succeed in their role.

If we want a new manager to have a good chance of being accepted by the team, it is preferable to involve them in the selection process, especially those who are going to report directly to the newcomer. You might think this is a bit risky. "Why let others encroach on my decision-making? They may interfere or put barriers in my way." "What if they don't like the person I want to hire?"

Yes, those risks exist. But it is better to take a little longer to find the right person, knowing that they will fit in and that they will be accepted by the team, than to hire whoever you initially prefer and then encounter resistance from within the team.

Resistance will lead to difficulties, causing delays as their new leader starts introducing changes and raising unnecessary fears in the personnel. The latent emotions within the department are also an important consideration. As in my example of the selection of the new FD, it is possible that the team had an attachment to the previous manager, or conversely that they are wary, having had a bad experience with him or her.

Allowing those who report to someone in a senior position to be involved in the recruitment process offers several advantages:

- They will feel empowered and motivated by having had a voice in the process.

- They will share some of the responsibility for the choice made.
- They will realise that it is necessary to make concessions during the selection process, thus managing their expectations.
- They will be more likely to do what they can to support the new manager and their success.

When others arbitrarily place something or someone in front of us, it is easy and tempting to pick faults.

⚠️ **WHEN WE HELP MAKE A DECISION, WE ARE MORE LIKELY TO SUPPORT THAT CHOICE AND PAY ATTENTION TO THE ADVANTAGES RATHER THAN THE SHORTCOMINGS.**

Involving people who would have the power to create considerable barriers in some decision-making is a smart investment.

In my story of the new FD, the three people who were to report to him participated in the selection and interview process. Therefore, when the new manager arrived, not only did they already know him, but they were keen for him to start a new chapter for the team.

I have used this approach on several occasions very successfully. If part of your job is to hire people-managers, why not try it, and see what results it gives you? You can also try this approach for other types of decisions; you will see how it is possible that those who you feared would create obstacles along the way, can become allies, involving them in your success, thanks to having their hand in the game.

ASKING FOR HELP WORKS

To get help, sometimes we just have to ask for it.

We have talked about how to involve others when we are at the definition stage of a project and decision-making as a strategy to get support, especially in cases where the interested parties will be affected by our actions.

In addition, there are other types of projects where it is not necessary to reach a consensus: we simply need the initiative or courage to ask for assistance. How many times have you not asked for something because you thought the answer was going to be no? Let's think about this, putting our ego aside for a moment. If we have already accepted a 'no', asking can only improve our chances.

> [!] **WHEN WE LEARN TO ACCEPT THE 'NO'S WITHOUT BEING DEJECTED OR OFFENDED, IT'S AMAZING HOW EASY IT CAN BE TO GET THINGS BY SIMPLY ASKING FOR THEM.**

When I started the process of changing my professional direction, from a CFO in a company to a consultant and mentor, I began to follow some renowned professionals on social networks who already did this type of work. One in particular had a good track record, thousands of followers and had already published two books. It occurred to me that having a conversation with him might be helpful, given my new aspirations. But why would this gentleman spend time with me when he knew nothing about me and had nothing to gain by doing so?

Nevertheless, I sent him a message on LinkedIn to say that a meeting with him would be very useful to me. And do you know what? The next day he wrote back and we arranged to meet. We held a video call that I found really valuable and he seemed to enjoy being able to support me at that time.

We have a hard time making requests openly to both acquaintances and strangers. The possible reasons are many: embarrassment, not wanting to be a nuisance or because we think that others will not want to provide us with the support we need. The truth is that there are times when we have absolutely nothing to lose. The next time you find yourself in this kind of situation and want something from someone, I encourage you to ask them. If you don't even ask, you already have a 'no'.

And if you still have doubts, ask yourself: what would your answer be if it was the other person who was asking you?

If the answer to your request turns out to be a no, or there is no answer at all, nothing happens. The only thing you risk is a little dent in your ego if you decide to take it that way. Besides, not asking for help at the right time often leads to failure.

> In chapter 8 I will tell you more on how to make the most of failure.

But there is another, more important reason why we need to learn to ask for support: our well-being, which we will talk about in the last part of this book. Asking for assistance is a way to get what we want and also taking care of ourselves.

> Think of a recent situation where you haven't asked for something you needed or that would have benefited you:

- Write down what you would have asked for and from whom.
- Make a list of the possible negative consequences that asking could have brought you.
- Make a list of possible benefits if that person had agreed to your request.
- Draw your own conclusions and act as you see fit.

MENTORS AND ALLIES

If you find people to guide and support you, you will reach your destination sooner.

Let's start with an exercise. Take a deep breath and think of the first person that comes to mind when you think of a mentor. Pay attention to the expression on your face and the feelings that this person has awakened in you.

There is a story I would like to use to illustrate this topic:

One night, a police officer found a man looking for his keys under a lamppost. He joined the man in his search, only to discover, after hours of searching, that the man had actually lost his keys in the nearby park.

"Then why are you looking here?" the officer asked.

"Because this is where the light is," the man replied.

This is known as the street lamp effect and it happens because our perspective is narrow and we tend look for things in the easiest place but where it is actually impossible for us to find them.

Mentoring could be described as a process of encouraging the protégé to look beyond the light of the lamppost.

> HAVING ONE OR MORE MENTORS THROUGHOUT YOUR CAREER CAN BRING YOU CLARITY IN MOMENTS OF DARKNESS, 'EUREKA' MOMENTS AND ACCELERATE OR IMPROVE YOUR PERSONAL AND PROFESSIONAL PROGRESSION.

A mentor is a trusted guide with relevant know-how - someone who shares their knowledge, skills and experience to promote the progression of another person. The mentoring process comprises many aspects for both parties involved.

The role of a mentor is not to tell you how they did it, what you should do, or how to do it. Mentoring conversations are there to prompt you to realise your own potential and see what you're capable of.

In my life and career, mentoring has taken many forms and not all of them were evident to me at the time. One of the best memories of mentoring I have is when before leaving the organisation, one of my line managers gave me a special parting gift. It was a book called 'The Prince' by Niccolò Machiavelli. When I read it, I realised that he was subtly giving me advice on how to manage my team and influence others, as there were many nuances about human behavior that I hadn't noticed.

The person being mentored receives counseling, their perspective is broadened and they become more motivated to increase their skills and accelerate their development.

The mentor fosters their sense of purpose by sharing their experience, contributing to others what they once received as they continue to grow.

Good mentoring is based on mutual learning, trust and inspiration.

In practice, for me, being a mentor is all about personal fulfillment. It is a form of participation that gives me satisfaction because I try to guide the people I support, drawing from some of the learning situations I have had which were, at that time, difficult to achieve. Thanks to this, the obstacles that I have encountered throughout my career have become of real value.

Mentoring is about giving and receiving. There are many ways to give and receive mentorship. A mentor can be a professional advisor or someone senior in your organisation. It can even be a younger person or junior colleague who is able to provide you with the advice and perspective you need at a particular point or situation.

To get the most out of a mentoring process, it is advisable to agree on a methodology, align your expectations, set goals and define how to measure success.

Mentoring is the result of a relationship between two people with the potential to add value to each other with different, but complementary roles. With honesty, communication and good intentions it is possible to see beyond the lamppost and turn mentoring into a good experience, just like the one that gave you those positive feelings about the mentor you remembered at the beginning of this topic.

After you have read this section, ask yourself and write:

- If you're already in a mentoring process, what more could you do to make the most of it?
- If you're not, why not start one?
- Write about people who have mentored you and what benefits or learnings they led to.
- Write about people you've mentored and any benefits or insight you gained.
- Think of someone you'd like to mentor you at the present time and write down your reasons.
- Think of someone whom you could mentor and write down your reasons.
- If you have any thoughts after the previous instructions, write them down.

Even if you're not a brand, you need a sponsor because another way to accelerate your progression is to have allies or admirers in positions of leadership and influence. As we saw in chapter 1, the fact that your boss thinks you are doing a good job is not enough for you to succeed within a company. We can establish strong links with people in positions of influence, but going one step further will make all the difference. And by that, I mean finding a sponsor within your present company or someone working in a completely different one but where you feel might be able to advance more successfully.

A SPONSOR PLAYS THE ROLE OF A MENTOR WITH ONE KEY DIFFERENCE: THERE IS AN EXPLICIT AGREEMENT BETWEEN YOU THAT THIS PERSON CAN, AND WANTS TO, HELP YOU PROGRESS IN THE ORGANISATION, IF YOUR CAPABILITIES WARRANT IT.

The first time I was told about this type of relationship in a leadership development program, I said to myself, "That's impossible. How embarrassing! How am I going to find someone who wants to sponsor me?"

In the end, doing so was much simpler than I had thought. As I explained in the previous section, there is a way: by asking.

I asked my boss's boss, who was the CFO of the Europe, Middle East and Africa (EMEA) region. He was also in the finance department and had a lot of influence in the organisation beyond the region I worked in. I liked him as a person and admired him as a professional. Also, although our encounters were only occasional, we always had relaxed interactions. Once I had identified him as a good candidate for the role of sponsor in my professional career, I plucked up the courage.

> If you have questions about how to prepare for the meeting, take a look at Chapter 2.

I carefully prepared notes about what I wanted from him and for what purpose.

I explained that I really liked his style and that his contributions as a sponsor, if he was willing to do so, would enrich my development. I also told him that in large organisations it is important to have people who know us well and will support us when opportunities for promotions come up. I didn't want special treatment or favoritism but I did want him to get to know me better and be aware of my aspirations and abilities. We agreed to meet once a quarter to work together on my development. I was delighted and so was he.

During that conversation we began a relationship that continues to this day. Over the next twelve months, with his help, my reputation and status within the organisation continued to grow. I was invited to be part of the EMEA Senior Leadership Team (SLT) which gave me access to more important platforms, including attending the EMEA regional conferences. Although we haven't worked in the same company for a few years now, he's someone I know I can turn to if I need advice or a recommendation.

If you don't have a sponsor yet, what are you waiting for?

Think about the contribution a sponsor could make to your career:

- Make a list of senior people in your organisation (or elsewhere) who could offer such advice and benefits.
- Analyse your current relationship with them by dividing the list into those whom you could approach now and those with whom you would need to develop the relationship a little further.
- On both sides of the list, mark the people who you truly admire and like.
- As a start, choose someone to approach and make the proposal. If you get any refusals, keep moving forward until you find a sponsor.

Chapter 4

TAKE THE REINS

I imagine that by now, although I haven't explicitly mentioned it, you've realised that being proactive plays an essential role in your ability to progress professionally and achieve your work goals.

To complete our journey about how to maximise results in managing the external world, we are left with several strategies which I realised - when I learned how to apply them and took the initiative unapologetically - had always been available to me.

I do not intend to review all the areas that require having this attitude because it will depend a lot on your personal circumstances but in this chapter we will talk about those areas where it is tempting to take a step back and yet are essential to our evolution. In particular:

- Communicating your personal value proposition.
- Balancing the relationship with your direct manager.
- Always being one step ahead.

COMMUNICATING YOUR VALUE PROPOSITION

Are you able to articulate your value proposition in a minute?

To progress in your career, it is not enough to wait for others to see the value in your contribution and demonstrate it by giving you that promotion, special project or salary increase.

> ⚠️ IF WE ARE NOT ABLE TO ARTICULATE OUR VALUE PROPOSITION PROPERLY AND AT THE RIGHT TIMES, WE CAN GO UNNOTICED AND LOSE OUT ON THOSE OPPORTUNITIES WE WANT AND DESERVE.

I confess that I have not always been very good at this, especially at the beginning of my career, but over the years I have realised its importance and I have learned to promote myself naturally and in a way I feel comfortable with.

You need to value yourself and be able to convey assertively - albeit without arrogance - what your strengths are in the workplace. Even if you tell yourself that you are too humble, polite or embarrassed, excuses such as these are worthless.

Some people find this self-promotion a natural thing which they do superbly. You may be one of them or, when you think about these people, you feel some aversion towards them. Regardless of which group you belong to, it's worth spending time defining and communicating your value proposition because in the workplace, and in general, others are going to do it and if you don't actively do likewise, you may miss opportunities.

If you haven't already, you need to learn to promote yourself and feel good about doing so. If you're wondering how to go about it:

> ⚠️ IDENTIFY YOUR STRENGTHS AND THOSE ATTRIBUTES AND BEHAVIORS THAT DIFFERENTIATE YOU FROM OTHERS IN THE WORKPLACE. HOW DO YOU SHINE?

> **YOU CAN USE ACADEMIC METHODS, SUCH AS CLIFTON'S STRENGTHS, IN GALLUP'S BOOK, 'DISCOVER YOUR STRENGTHS' AND SEEK FEEDBACK FROM PEOPLE AROUND YOU.**

> In chapter 7 you will find ideas and exercises for you to identify the characteristics others recognise in you the most.

Try to identify personal images or stories to reinforce the impression of yourself that you want to communicate. This will increase your beliefs around your self-worth. It is easier to value the contribution of others than our own, even when what we admire in them is also within us. Think about how easy it is to admire others for what they are good at or the things they do:

> **OUR STRENGTHS AND DIFFERENT ATTRIBUTES MAY BE MORE EVIDENT TO OTHERS THAN THEY ARE TO OURSELVES.**

Once you have clarity about your best qualities as a person and professionally, find words and phrases to craft a personal pitch that allows you to communicate your 'individual value proposition' to your boss, your team, your network, potential employers and many more so that you can convey those ideas on your curriculum vitae, in presentations, at interviews and in other opportunities which arise.

> A pitch is summary or presentation that is made for the purpose of selling or persuading.

It's about being selective - not about telling everyone everything about yourself. If others need more details, they will ask. When in doubt, remind yourself that 'less is more' and always choose to mention those aspects which truly characterise you, whilst trying to avoid clichés.

Be subtle with those messages. Practice by intertwining your pitch in conversations, even if you only include it in part. This will make it easier for you to communicate, finding the right words for you and adapting them to be used in different contexts, both written and verbal.

For example, my value proposition as I write these lines is: "I share my personal and professional experience with professionals, entrepreneurs and businesses, accompanying them as they take the necessary steps to reach their potential. I provide consultancy tailored to specific projects, via regular support within the business or personal mentoring. My speciality is change, with particular expertise in finance, business transformation and the engagement of people." The words I use change when I tell a potential client or acquaintance in person, but I stay true to those particular aspects that set me apart from the rest.

> ⚠️ **YOUR VALUE PROPOSITION IS SOMETHING ALIVE THAT EVOLVES WITH YOU DEPENDING ON YOUR STYLE, EXPERIENCE, ORGANISATION AND THE PRESENT MOMENT.**

I recommend that you develop several different personal value propositions for different audiences. For example, the value proposition illustration I outlined earlier was generic and is useful for potential clients or people who don't have a specific role in my interactions with them.

The value proposition we would choose for a team member, or for our line manager, would be different and would include aspects that are relevant to them from their perspective. You would talk to a member of your team about what leadership style characterises you and how they can communicate with you so that you work effectively together.

Or for a headhunter, for example, I would introduce myself along the lines of, "I am a natural entrepreneur and during my career I have taken advantage of change to develop and progress until I became a CFO. I am passionate about communicating and I am a leader of people with a collaborative and approachable style. I have had the opportunity of working within multicultural working groups in multinational companies in several countries."

> ⚠️ DELIVERING THE RIGHT MESSAGES WILL HELP YOU TO GET THOSE OPPORTUNITIES AND MAKE SURE THAT YOU AND THE PEOPLE AROUND YOU ARE AWARE OF THE VALUE YOU BRING TO THE ORGANISATION.

Do not leave your personal brand solely in the hands of others. Take the reins to define it and communicate it properly and consistently, at the appropriate times. Ask yourself:

- How good am I at marketing myself?

Develop a pitch about your value proposition:

- Make a list of the key ideas you want to convey.
- Of these, choose four or five that are particularly noticeable.
- Create a paragraph of no more than a hundred words including all of those key ideas.
- Summarise the previous paragraph in two sentences, discarding those elements that, although important, are not quite as differentiating.
- Create one generic summary and another adapted to a particular group of interest, given your current situation, such as headhunters, investors, etc.
- Put into practice communicating these messages during the next few days. For example:
  - Take advantage when talking to a friend.
  - Use them when you introduce yourself to someone in the office.
  - Include these points on a slide which you can use to introduce yourself at the beginning of a presentation.

BALANCING THE RELATIONSHIP WITH YOUR DIRECT MANAGER

In some cultures, it is believed that bosses are responsible for taking the initiative, leading, commanding, and setting boundaries. Subordinates are supposed to follow instructions, be prudent with

what they say and adapt to the style of their superiors. These examples are somewhat extreme on purpose to illustrate that, in those cultures or situations, the 'balance of power' is not, in fact, balanced.

Your ability to effect a real balance will depend in part on the environment in which you operate, as well as your personal style and that of your direct superior. However, if you act with initiative to even out the imbalance as much as possible, you will have more influence and accelerate your professional career.

You can help even out the imbalance by taking four steps:

- Establish mutual responsibilities.
- Separate the person from the tasks.
- Find your voice.
- Promote one-to-one interactions.

ESTABLISHING MUTUAL RESPONSIBILITIES

> 〔!〕 AN EMPLOYMENT RELATIONSHIP INVOLVES AN EXCHANGE BETWEEN TWO PARTIES WITH DISTINCT BUT MUTUAL RESPONSIBILITIES.

When we lack confidence or operate within certain corporate cultures, we forget that there is more than one participant in that exchange.

Good leaders set their expectations clearly. They assist their team members in the fulfillment of their function by establishing objectives and clearly communicating of the rules of the game. These being made clear, their teams are able to act accordingly and carry out what is necessary, as well as avoid misunderstandings and unnecessary friction.

Therefore, as a member of a team, you can also reap benefits by communicating your expectations and needs in order to achieve success in your work and maximise the support you get from your superior. It is not about giving your direct manager a list of your demands but about expressing how that person can support you to be more effective in your work and feel better about your interactions with them.

It is up to you to complete your tasks and manage your area of responsibility. At the same time, your direct superior is responsible for guiding you, sharing their knowledge and providing the tools and resources necessary for you to fully deliver what is expected of you.

The best time to set the working methods that are useful in your relationship with your manager is at the beginning of the relationship. I recommend that it should be one of the first conversations you have with a new boss or client. Even if that hasn't been possible in the past, it's always a good time to start.

If you are not assertive in being explicit about your needs to your line manager, you will lose not only the ability to do your job properly but also opportunities for growth and personal satisfaction.

SEPARATING THE PERSON FROM THE TASKS

There is a very helpful book by Miguel Ruiz which I recommend, called 'The Four Agreements', which lays out four basic agreements one can live by, in order to avoid suffering. One of those agreements is, "Don't take anything personally."

It's easy to forget that interactions with our superiors or with our direct team concern a number of tasks or organizational needs. Those tasks or needs have nothing to do with them as individuals. Of course, each person has a big role to play in how the challenges that arise are managed but, that said, it's essential to remember that the person who is your direct superior and the job they must do are two different components and don't always need to be linked.

I have worked in many organizations and have been responsible for large teams, sometimes including people who were my friends outside of work. Learning to separate the two facets of these relationships has helped me to do my job well but also take care of those important personal bonds and maintain them over time beyond our common professional interactions.

I've had to make hard choices and do things that I disliked in my role as a leader. That hasn't meant that I didn't appreciate the impact I was creating or that I didn't care for the people who were affected by those difficult decisions.

Throughout my professional career I have had to fire people due to decisions made by others and sometimes by myself, when I believed that dismissal was the right course of action for the organization and for the individual involved. On more than one occasion, at the end of a redundancy meeting, the person I had just fired has given me a hug because, although I had just given them bad news, we were able to acknowledge the difference between what I did as part of my job and our feelings as people and colleagues.

If we take these two dimensions into account and strive to take care of them separately, we can manage the boss-subordinate relationship more effectively, thus creating an equilibrium in the balance of power that we need.

FINDING YOUR VOICE

We've talked about conflict management and the methodology you can use during difficult conversations. Being able to express our needs and feelings properly not only enriches work relationships, but also personal ones.

In order to express ourselves frankly to our superiors, we need to feel safe and heard. To feel safe, we need confidence, and this trust requires good communication accompanied by actions that support that feeling. All of this takes time and effort from both sides.

In several of my roles I have observed how some colleagues always agreed with the person in charge but, as soon as they left, they vented some very different opinions. By finding our voice, we create coherence between what we express and what we do.

Always agreeing with your line manager denotes a lack of both transparency and trust.

> ⚠️ BY BEING OPEN ABOUT OUR TRUE OPINIONS WE CAN EARN THE RESPECT OF DIRECT SUPERIORS, WHICH BALANCES THE SCALE OF POWER.

PROMOTING ONE-ON-ONE INTERACTIONS

With the three steps above, the gap between superior and subordinate narrows. This increases confidence in the subordinate's ability to take on more responsibility in their position or their possible promotion to another.

Don't sabotage yourself, devaluing yourself unnecessarily. For example, there are people who have such a helpful attitude that they inadvertently minimise their own status towards others; for example, volunteering to take the minutes at the meeting or make the coffee.

I remember one of my colleagues who, despite being clearly capable, could not earn the respect of our common line manager. We were both directors and yet she was constantly interrupted by him during her presentations, even to the point of his taking over completely. Without realizing it, her attitude contributed to the lack of trust and appreciation that our boss felt towards her.

Each conversation can be approached with an attitude of collaboration and equality, while maintaining the appropriate distance.

Being able to find solutions to obstacles along the way is undoubtedly a necessary aspect to taking on more responsibility. When we are able to bring solutions to the table, we are more effective, more self-sufficient and generate more trust from others.

Even if we do not have a position of responsibility, it is possible to enhance this capability in many ways.

Think about options. When a problem arises, it's tempting to seek help or let others come up with the solutions. However, even when it is not our responsibility, it helps to think about what possible solutions may exist. There is a big difference between reporting a problem to someone, who may be able to help you, saying "There is a problem," and, "There is a problem, but a possible solution could be...". Although sometimes finding viable solutions is not easy, if we do not even try, we will never be able to build this capability.

In my experience as head of the department, I have observed the differences in attitude among my team members. Those who came armed with opinions and possible solutions to the challenges they encountered have been the ones I have trusted and valued the most, as individuals with talent and the capacity for progression. It's easy to settle into letting our superiors take the initiative but, if you want to progress, you have to show that the matters you are entrusted with are in good hands, possibly even better than theirs.

Think about your relationship with your manager or whoever you report directly or indirectly to:

- On a scale of 1 to 10, how would you describe the balance of power in your interactions with them? 1 being "Completely unbalanced" and 10 "Completely balanced".
    - What aspects currently contribute to the imbalance (if any)?
    - What steps can you take to improve such balance?
- Think about a problematic situation or incident you've faced recently.
    - Describe how you presented the scenario to your direct superior.
    - Did you provide possible solutions when communicating the incident?
- Think of a recent meeting with your manager in which you disagreed or did not like their position.
    - How did you behave?
    - What could you have done differently?
- Write down what you've become aware of doing this exercise and write down possible actions you can take in the future to improve your balance of power.

ALWAYS BEING ONE STEP AHEAD

This topic, which ends the environment section in this first part of the book, may seem extremely obvious, but taking care of these core elements — going back to basics — can give you a real advantage in the chaotic environments we navigate. Preparation and organization are key elements for the good execution of any performance and, as you move up in your professional career, it will be the best way to obtain results through others.

Within this remit there are four areas worth considering:

- The effort you put into informing yourself properly.
- The space you create to reflect and assess certain situations.
- Your self-discipline and methods to prepare meetings properly.
- Your ability to call others and yourself into action.

INFORM YOURSELF

It seems simple, but being well informed is more difficult than it seems. In previous chapters we've talked about how, through our interactions with others, we discover information that can change our perspective.

If we draw conclusions or act after considering incomplete scenarios, we can have a detrimental effect on the situation by: misinterpreting information, being unfair to others, rushing, etc.

WHEN FACED WITH A NEW SITUATION, FIND OUT AS MUCH AS POSSIBLE BEFORE DRAWING CONCLUSIONS OR CONVEYING THE MESSAGE TO YOUR SUPERIOR.

That will show that you have a broad view of the circumstances and that you think beyond the specific details.

The necessary information isn't going to come to you on its own, so it's essential that you're able to ask the right questions. These questions are important whether someone comes to you with a problem or it is something you discover independently.

When I was the director of financial control in a multinational company in London, I began to suspect that a debt owed to the company was included on the balance sheet but which we had no chance of ever being paid. Confirming that the balance was correct and that we could count on that money being receivable was my responsibility, so I had to do something about that suspicion.

There is information that, when we share it with others, can bring us more problems than advantages. Here are some questions that will help you gather the necessary information, using the example of my discovery of erroneous balances. They are not exhaustive but they will help you discover others that may be relevant in your particular circumstances.

- What magnitude are we talking about? There is a world of difference between communicating to your superior that there is an error of 1,000 pounds and telling them that the figure is 20 million.
- Is it a one-off or widespread? It is a different matter if the erroneous balances are specific to some accounts than if there are errors which affect all the accounts.
- What failure has led to the errors? There is a big difference between an error made when processing a particular contract and a pervasive error which has affected many transactions.
- How long has this been happening?
- Has the original issue been fixed yet or is it still happening?
- What possible solutions do you have?
- How difficult is it to mitigate the impact?
- How does this information affect the person receiving it? It requires a much more careful approach to communicate a failure to the person responsible for the error than it would be to someone unconnected to the cause of the problem.

In the case of my discovery, I had to report that a loss of many millions needed to be recognised and, as you can imagine, that information was not going to be liked by anyone so I had to establish all of the facts before making a move.

The way we gather evidence depends, of course, on each case but one thing is clear: the more information we have, the better we will manage the situation and make a good impression on others regarding our management abilities.

Think of a recent incident where you have suffered negative consequences because you didn't collect enough information or had erroneous information.

- Write down what questions you could have asked to get the information that would have prevented what happened.
- Write about what you could have done differently or how you will manage a similar situation in the future.

REFLECT

Finding the time to think is a great investment. It is beneficial to your personal well-being, which we will talk about in the second part of the book, and will also improve how you manage relationships, your work and your ability to take on more responsibility.

We are the main obstacle if we do not create the right habits. Give yourself time to think by creating spaces in your diary. For example, dedicate a few minutes before meetings to organise your ideas or blocking time so you can digest issues that concern you.

One of my line managers, from whom I learned a lot about this, always prepared meetings thoroughly. The extent of her preparation was evident with each sentence that she said and noticeable because she often took the lead in meetings. That control and poise are not achieved by improvising at every turn. It requires patience, intellectual work and concentration.

Thinking things through carefully also allows us to be more selective with what information we share with others and what we don't. It helps us to decide what information adds value if we share it, even if it is not sensitive, and what does not.

> [!] THERE IS AN OPTIMAL BALANCE BETWEEN TRANSPARENCY AND DISCRETION. LEARNING TO BE SELECTIVE WITH THE INFORMATION WE SHARE CAN SAVE US HEADACHES.

For example, in the private sector, one of the most damaging pieces of information that can fall into people's hands is salary information about their colleagues. Even in cases where the pay gap is more than justified because of the role definition, experience or other characteristics, people are invariably compelled to make comparisons - and comparisons are destructive. I have seen, on many occasions, how someone who was previously perfectly happy with their salary suddenly loses motivation and feels aggrieved because they find out about a colleague's pay, even when their position is more senior.

> [!] WHEN SHARING INFORMATION ADDS NOTHING OF VALUE, IT IS SMARTER NOT TO SHARE IT UNLESS IT IS REALLY NECESSARY FOR THE SITUATION.

Being prepared is essential if you want to reach the top. You need to have time to think about what you want to communicate or put in place, anticipating possible reactions and the needs of others.

GET ORGANISED

How many times have you entered a meeting without being clear about what it was about? If there are many, stop it right now!

In many work environments we spend hours in meetings. Meetings are black holes of time. A meeting that does not bear fruit is not only a waste of time and resources but also a source of frustration.

Whether we are the organisers or are invited, being clear about what the purpose of the meeting is before you attend is key, enabling you to ensure that it is productive and makes a real contribution.

If you are invited to a meeting and you are not clear about the objectives, ask what they are before accepting. If you are the one who initiates it, clearly define what your intentions are and draw up an agenda.

AGREE ON NEXT STEPS

How many times have you left a meeting without knowing precisely what you need to do or without having clearly assigned actions and responsibility to others? If there are many, you know what I'd suggest ...

Jokes aside, to be effective as team members or leaders, it is necessary to clarify action points, tasks, responsibilities and timelines. If you tie up the loose ends, your performance and that of others involved will be far more efficient. So, if you want to go far on the professional ladder, this simple discipline will be very valuable.

The concept of going one step ahead is a good place at which to conclude this section on how to manage our environment.

> **⚠ BY BEING PROACTIVE IN HOLDING THE REINS, TAKING CARE OF RELATIONSHIPS AND MANAGING CONFLICT, YOU CAN OVERCOME MANY OF THE OBSTACLES IN YOUR PROFESSIONAL CAREER.**

Think of meetings or encounters you have recently had that have frustrated you, resulted in a waste of time, or in which you have not achieved your purpose:

- Choose an occasion when you were invited to a meeting and write about what you could have done differently, before or during the meeting, to make it more productive.
- Choose an occasion when you promoted the meeting and write about what you could have done differently, before or during the meeting, to make it more productive.
- Set your intentions to manage these aspects more effectively from now on.

DEVELOPMENT

In the first four chapters we have addressed common situations and the steps you can take to manage the relationships in your environment to get the most out of your performance.

Now we will begin to address how you can value and strengthen your own growth so that you continue to develop and thus be able to reach your full potential.

Chapter 5

CHANGE IS THE WAY

"The only thing that is constant is change." Heraclitus.

Life is about transformation and our ability to not only to deal with it, but to make the most of it, is an important key to success. I love change and I have sought to evolve throughout my life. Now that I'm in my forties, I realise that for a long time I had been following my intuition and looking for new paths when I no longer felt good about something.

> 🛈 CHANGE IS A REALITY OF EXISTENCE ON OUR LIFE'S JOURNEY, SO THE BETTER WE APPROACH & ADAPT TO THESE TRANSFORMATIONS, THE MORE WE WILL GET OUT OF LIFE.

IDENTIFY THE TYPE

In the course of our lives, we encounter some changes that we readily welcome, some which we reluctantly accept and others which we would prefer to avoid. With these dividing lines, we could divide the situations of change into three groups because the strategies we can use to manage them sets them apart. Let's give them nicknames:

- "Gifts" - those we desire.
- "Earthquakes" - because they are inevitable.
- "Plunges" - because, although we want them, we have to throw ourselves in.

Gifts are the least problematic. It does not matter if we voluntarily seek something we want or if it falls from the sky; changes that are appealing tend to be welcome. Of course, there is always tension until we get used to it but, in general, we gladly adapt to new situations which we perceive to be desirable. I would say that the strategy for this kind of change is simply to enjoy it and make the most of it.

Earthquakes represent changes that are inevitable, whether for better or for worse. This kind of change is out of our control so there's nothing to be gained from resisting it. If it's something we don't want — losing a job, our boss resigning, being left by the person we're in love with — we can be proactive in taking steps to mitigate the turmoil, but only when we've accepted the situation.

Acceptance is not the same as admitting defeat: it is the recognition that something has moved in a certain direction and will not change. Of course, it's hard to let go of things when we don't want them to change, such as the death of a loved one or abandonment from someone we love. We waste a lot of energy in the first parts of the five stages of grief (denial, anger, negotiation, depression, and acceptance) instead of managing it advantageously so that we can get on with our lives happily.

Often, issues that we perceive to be negative when they happen give rise to positive outcomes. I have thousands of examples of challenges that fit into this category and I am sure that you can also remember many from your own experience.

Plunges are the most complicated changes and the ones that deserve the most attention.

> 🗨 THOSE CHANGES WE CAN AVOID ARE THE HARDEST TO SURMOUNT, BUT CAN HOLD LIFE'S BEST OPPORTUNITIES.

Among the opportunities that taking the plunge can give us, is the chance to step out of our comfort zone and pursue challenges that, whilst difficult, will make us better people and enable us to achieve goals that will surprise us - and others, too.

When we are reluctant to change and unable to overcome a blockage, we can end up massively immersed in routine. It can be difficult and scary to make modifications that are not strictly necessary, especially when there are risks involved and we need to swim upstream to take the plunge and make it happen.

LISTEN TO AND ACT ON YOUR INSTINCT

This may sound a bit esoteric, but the hardest thing may be to realise that it's the right time to change. We are all experts at suppressing emotions, finding reasons to maintain the status quo and justify it to ourselves.

My experience suggests that despondency may have something to do with a person's inability to carry out the evolution necessary to be in balance with what they need.

> 🗨 WHEN WE HAVE EMOTIONAL DISCOMFORT, THOSE FEELINGS ARE A SIGN OF SOMETHING NOT BEING RIGHT AND TO ELIMINATE THAT TROUBLE, SOMETHING NEEDS TO BE CHANGED.

We deceive ourselves, sometimes because we don't want to do what is necessary and sometimes because we can't recognise the source of our discomfort. It is not always easy to identify what exactly it is that we need to change but, with a little research, it is usually possible to find out. At times, we put the blame on factors that eventually turn out to be irrelevant.

There is no single, powerful and simple question I can recommend to enable you to find out quickly what the problem is or what to do, but your inner self does know. If you listen carefully, you'll be able to figure it out. So ask yourself:

⚠ ARE MY THOUGHTS IN ACCORDANCE WITH MY EMOTIONS?

Something as simple as reading these words or listening to someone else can stimulate revealing thoughts.

If those thoughts are accompanied by a sense of clarity and deep knowledge, you'll know you've hit the jackpot.

One of the hardest decisions I've ever had to make was to separate from my husband after more than twenty years together. I was uneasy for quite a while - stressed and sleepless. I used to cry in the shower but I didn't really know what was wrong with me. Some would say that it's just a mid-life crisis. Maybe, but during the process there came a time when I simply knew what was wrong, even though my rational mind tried to persuade me otherwise at every turn. For that reason, I would tell you to listen to that inner instinct and not always take the reasoning that your intellect offers you at face value.

One of the best pieces of advice I received during that period came from my boss at the time. It had been a while since I had been myself and he asked me one day:

"Are you okay?"

"Not really," I said, "I have a problem because something in my head is telling me to do one thing and my instinct another."

The wisdom in his answer shook me:

"If you need to do a SWOT analysis to make a personal decision, then you have a problem."

He was absolutely right.

> A SWOT is a tool used in companies to assess their situation in the market and help define their strategy. The name comes from the letters of each area that is analyzed: strengths, weaknesses, opportunities and threats.

> [!] RATIONAL EVALUATIONS OF COURSE HAVE A ROLE TO PLAY IN OUR LIVES WHEN MAKING DECISIONS BUT THERE IS ANOTHER DIMENSION TO CONSIDER THAT IS NOT FOUND IN RATIONAL MODELS.

> [!] THAT DIMENSION ENCOMPASSES FEELINGS AND DESIRES THAT, WHILE THEY MAY NOT BE RATIONAL AT ALL, HAVE AN ENORMOUS IMPACT ON OUR LIVES.

MAKE A DECISION

This is not straightforward because of the difficulty involved in determining what the right direction is. This step is difficult because it requires courage. Let's start with the bad news: once we figure out what 'plunge' we want to take and, until we arm ourselves with the courage to make the decision, we are dragged along a miserable journey, full of repetitive thoughts and doubts. This will only be alleviated by making the decision to make the change.

> [!] ONCE WE KNOW, WE CAN'T FORGET WHAT'S WRONG, SO THE LONGER WE ARE IN THIS PHASE, THE MORE WORN OUT WE'LL END UP.

Some people may get stuck in this 'knowing without acting' for a long time. Perhaps you know exactly what I mean if I ask if you can recall a time when you almost made the decision and then, the next day, you backed down.

That's not making a decision; it's making it difficult for ourselves. When you make the real decision, you know it because you feel a huge sense of relief. Even without having done anything yet, you feel like you *have* done it.

> 🔔 THE DAY WE MAKE THE DECISION WE START TO RELAX AGAIN AND MANY OF THE REASONS THAT HAVE MADE THE PROCESS DIFFICULT FOR US, SUDDENLY LOSE THEIR STRENGTH.

I have made the decision to leave a job on several occasions and I distinctly remember that the morning after making a final decision to leave, everything became easier again. What had affected me so much before, no longer did so and I even started enjoying the role again during my notice period.

When what we want seems too difficult to achieve, we can start the process by asking for help or simply talking to someone we trust to explore our options.

> 📝 Remember the keys to asking for help in Chapter 3.

Even if there are significant obstacles in our way, when we actually make the decision, we begin to see the light at the end of the tunnel. Our perspective changes and we are able to draw up a plan that, step by step, brings us closer to the goal, even if we still have a long way to go.

MAKE IT HAPPEN

Once the decision is made, the sooner we implement the change, the better.

> 🔔 SOME DECISIONS ARE HARDER TO EXECUTE THAN OTHERS BUT THERE'S NOTHING THAT A GOOD STEP-BY-STEP PLAN CAN'T PLOUGH THROUGH. SO MAKE A LIST, START AT THE BEGINNING AND MAKE IT HAPPEN.

It may seem like a cliché with my background in finance, but I've often used spreadsheets to manage personal plans, whether it's finding a place to live in a new city, a school for my kids, or a new job. Having the discipline to break it down into small steps and make some progress every day is a pretty foolproof way to achieve our purpose.

In 2007, just before the 2008 financial crisis, I quit my job and said to my boss at the time, "I don't know exactly what project I'll be undertaking. I just know that I feel like I need a project of my own." I love to cook and I had often thought about starting a business around food but despite this, without realising it, in less than two weeks I had bought a new laptop and began to draw up a blue-print of what my tax advisory business would be like. The document I wrote, to sort out my ideas and conceptualise the business, ended up becoming the 'welcome manual' and website for the clients of the company I started and named Rose & Clavel.

When I was taking those first steps I had many obstacles ahead: I had never had my own business, I had only been back in Spain for two years after many years in the UK, my local network was limited, and I lived in a competitive marketplace where businesses were frequently starting up, only to collapse a very short time afterwards.

Four years later, we had created a viable firm, recognised and valued by the local community, with more than two hundred clients and a team of twelve people. During those years I learned from and enjoyed the journey a great deal. When my personal circumstances changed and I wanted to change trajectory once again, I had to face many barriers: an escalating crisis in the market, responsibilities towards employees and customers – including my sister, who worked in the company – significant difficulty in selling that type of business ... and yet, voilà! I found a buyer for the business and everything went well less than three months after making the decision. This, of course, was the result of the initiative I took to overcome the barriers in my way.

⚠ DESPITE ANY APPARENT DIFFICULTIES IN MAKING SOME CHANGES, IF YOU GET DOWN TO WORK, YOU CAN MAKE THEM A REALITY. IT'S BETTER TO FAIL THAN TO THROW IN THE TOWEL BEFORE YOU START. YOU HAVE NOTHING TO LOSE BY TRYING.

In chapter 8 I will tell you how to take advantage of failure.

LOOK FORWARD

⚠ ONCE THE CHANGE IS MADE, WHETHER THE DECISION WAS CORRECT OR NOT IS SOMETHING THAT BECOMES IRRELEVANT.

⚠ DO NOT WASTE TIME OR ENERGY HESITATING. FOCUS ON IMPROVING ELEMENTS THAT CAN OPTIMISE THE END RESULT.

If there are issues that are not quite right, it is within our power to act. It is also useful to remind ourselves, as we said at the beginning, that transformations are and will continue to be constant. For that reason, even if the outcome is not exactly as we planned, there will certainly be pleasant surprises in the wake of this new path before another opportunity for evolution arrives.

IF YOU LEAD A TEAM, MAKE THEM PART OF IT

Another important part of change management has to do with how we take into account the circumstances and environment of others who are affected. It's great to learn how to personally deal with the transformations we initiate but, as leaders of a work group or in the family, our ability to take people from that environment on our journey is essential.

If it is difficult for us to take the plunge, imagine what it must be like for others. Have you ever sat by the side of a swimming pool, thinking about getting into the water, when someone sneaks up behind you and pushes you in? In our company or group environments, change may be dictated by the corporate strategy or by another department and are not welcome. In my experience, people don't react well to new system implementations, having a new line manager, or changing the way they work. This is because, although transformation can bring benefits later on, making it a reality during the execution phase is almost always difficult.

> 🗨 WHEN WE ARE IN A POSITION OF POWER AND INFLUENCE, AND OTHERS ARE AFFECTED BY THE CHANGES WE WANT OR NEED TO IMPLEMENT, IT IS OUR RESPONSIBILITY TO ENCOURAGE THE PEOPLE ON THE TEAM DURING THAT PROCESS OF EVOLUTION.

If we do so, they will feel happier and more motivated because we have managed the transformation carefully and with sensitivity towards their needs and realities. Here are some things you can think about to encourage your team members to join in that journey of change:

First, make them feel involved, if possible, at an early stage when you are still defining the solution. If you are drafting alterations over which you do have control, it is a good idea to organise a group session that allows you to think together about the possible options that could solve the problem and how they could be carried out. This can slow down the first part of the process and may result in compromises being made to keep the team on board. The advantage, though, is that you will probably end up with a solution born out of a broader vision and will therefore be more successful. Engaging people in this stage of the process will make them feel like they have played their part so they are more likely to help rather than hinder its implementation.

> 🗨 ENCOURAGING PEOPLE TO SAY WHAT THEY THINK CAN HELP TO MAKE IMPROVEMENTS, FIND NEW SOLUTIONS, TEST IDEAS, MAKE MISTAKES, AND FIND SOLUTIONS TO THE SITUATION. IT IS ALSO PART OF THE CHANGE PROCESS.

SAVE YOUR OBJECTIONS

Recognising the challenges that change could bring and proposing solutions is key, but your suggestions should not be expressed in an openly critical or resistant way. Don't reject the new ideas out of hand because if you openly refuse to adapt, you're effectively saying to your team that the effort that comes with change isn't worth it. The result is that you'll fail before you have even started. For a successful implementation, you'll need the cooperation and involvement of the people around you, so don't let yourself be too easily dejected at the first hurdle.

If you are not the person responsible for carrying out alterations imposed on you, it is also important that you are discreet with your objections.

> ⚠️ YOU WILL ONLY ADD VALUE IF YOU SHARE YOUR CONCERNS AND PROPOSALS FOR IMPROVEMENT WITH THOSE WHO HAVE INFLUENCE OVER THE OUTCOMES.

> ⚠️ SHARING SKEPTICISM OPENLY WITH YOUR PEERS ONLY GENERATES DISCOMFORT AND NEGATIVELY CONTAMINATES A SCENE THAT CAN ALREADY BE TRICKY.

When you openly resist transformations, ask yourself, "Does what I am saying add any value or am I just venting my frustrations?" If you need to let off steam, do it in your own time, not at work. There is nothing better than venting your annoyance and/or frustration over a beer with a friend.

ONE STEP AT A TIME

Start small if possible. Do a trial or pilot run. Most evolutionary processes are divisible into smaller components. For example, if you plan to change the execution of a specific process, instead of making all the alterations simultaneously, start perhaps with a single client or case. This is sensible because after many years of experiencing changes in organizations, I have never witnessed a solution which was perfectly defined from the outset. By testing the modification or doing a trial run, you will learn a lot and therefore be able to revise your plan before carrying out the implementation in full. Also, if circumstances change or some parts are cancelled, it will not be a total waste of time and resources.

CURB YOUR ENTHUSIASM

Do not be too ambitious. Beware of getting carried away with your initial ideas and immediately following it up with, "Well, now we're on a roll, let's also re-structure this!" Never-ending goals are the worst enemy of any project, as the wish list can grow out of control. A common problem is that it can be difficult to isolate individual elements. For that reason, it is tempting to keep dreaming and adding new aspirations willy-nilly. However, if we keep our feet on the ground, even if we cannot save the world, we can protect the change we seek.

LOOK OUTWARDS

Think about the impact your changes will have on areas outside of your control. How will it affect other parts of the organization or group? Few transformations can be implemented in total isolation. Proposals that make a lot of sense from the perspective of your immediate environment can cause a lot of problems in other parts of the organization. This means having empathy beyond your own group and considering adapting some aspects to mitigate possible negative effects elsewhere. This may involve modifying the plan or simply keeping the necessary people informed.

STOP TO ALLOW CHANGE

I have observed many times how new managers often launch new initiatives as soon as they arrive, but that plan rarely includes discontinuing many existing methods. It's not a good idea to overload a team with new activities and processes without adapting or removing some of what still remains.

One way to help you become more effective is to eliminate tasks that no longer provide the value they once did. Of course, change necessitates adding new activities but also removing those that no longer make sense, so you may ask yourself: which tasks are not strictly necessary and can be eliminated to mitigate the impact of the rest of the activities?

PAY ATTENTION TO COMMUNICATION

Communication is extremely important before, during and after any process of transformation. Many of the initiatives I've seen in organisations have struggled due to a poor communication strategy which significantly weakened large projects.

Unfortunately, it is not easy to communicate well. It is not enough to send an email, display a notice or publish it on the intranet. It's about having multiple ways to reach different people across the organization.

We often define communications from our perspective, so we shouldn't be surprised when they're not well received by the audience. In order to do this well, we need to consider the different groups of people and how they are affected by the change and adapt the communication style to their circumstances. Some people will benefit from a face-to-face conversation, while others will only need to be informed in a less personalised way. I've learned that people don't always listen or read, so you may need several ways to convey the message you want appropriately to the relevant parties.

Think of a change that you are, or have been, responsible for bringing about. It can be something work or personal:

- Describe the change in a few words.
- What behaviors or attitudes can help you make it happen?
- What can you do differently to make the people around you accept or adapt to such evolution?
- What can you stop doing to remove obstacles to that transformation?
- Considering all the ideas covered by the previous points, write a brief conclusion of the situation.

ATTITUDE IS EVERYTHING

We have talked about the three types of change and what possible strategies we can use to make even the most complex of changes a reality. However, not all of these strategies will be effective unless your own attitude towards change is the right one. So now it's time to look in the mirror and ask yourself:

- What attitude do I have towards change?
- Do I avoid it or embrace it?

There is much written about transformation, its phases and how difficult it can be for people and organizations.

I consider myself a champion of change, determined to welcome change when presented with it, instead of avoiding it or going through those futile stages to which I have alluded.

> ⚠ **WHEN WE DON'T FEEL GOOD IN OUR PRIVATE LIVES OR FACE ORGANISATIONAL PROBLEMS, EVOLUTION IS THE ONLY PATH TO RESOLUTION.**

Organisations, like people, develop problems. Such dysfunctions affect everyone who is part of that system. Of course, the effects vary depending on the person, as not everyone is affected in the same way, but change is the solution, even if it has challenging consequences in themselves.

> ⚠ **WHEN WE DEVELOP AN ATTITUDE AS CHAMPIONS OF CHANGE, EMBRACING THE INEVITABLE PROCESS OF EVOLUTION, THE EXPERIENCE CAN GIVE US MORE THAN IT TAKES AWAY.**

I remember many situations in the office where people were kicking and screaming through the many initiatives that were brought to their table. That attitude only brought them frustration and worry, as well as diminishing their reputation in the organization.

If you still find that you do not embrace changes around you readily, I would like to remind you of some of the advantages that it can bring.

ENERGY AND ENTHUSIASM

Undertaking an evolutionary process with the right attitude gives us a great source of energy and the desire to succeed in a different phase. Unfamiliar things are stimulating and the paths taken in new territory can be, although challenging at times, enriching.

LEARNING AND TRAINING

Every development process involves going through a learning curve. It gives us the opportunity to add new technical skills, soft skills and know-how to our personal toolbox. Even the most traumatic turns bring us deep learning that will always be with us. As we experience them, we become stronger, more capable, and more resilient.

PEOPLE AND OPPORTUNITIES

When we change, we do new things and new people come into our lives, each with different interactions, whether brief and casual or deep and long lasting - new friendships, loves, teachers. And those people bring new opportunities - experiences, situations, jobs or projects that, without that turn, would have never arrived.

> [!] OUR DEVELOPMENT AS PEOPLE IS LINKED TO OUR ABILITY TO MANAGE CHANGE.

Living is changing, so the decision is yours. Do you want to live at your fullest, like a champion for change, or do you want to watch from behind the scenes as a mere observer, regretting each lost opportunity? The choice is yours.

And now I will throw you a boomerang because, after having encouraged you to embrace change, there remains an important question.

When the emotion that motivates us to change is fear or 'because I don't like it' instead of enthusiasm to start a new journey, it is possible that over time we will find ourselves still dealing with the same uncomfortable and outdated living patterns. So ask yourself:

- What basic emotion feeds my discomfort?

In chapter 13 we will open the can of worms of emotions.

Think of a recent or current situation in which you have resisted a significant change in your work or personal life:

- Describe the scene in a few words.
- Write about the energy and enthusiasm you've experienced in another change you perceived as good when it first happened. What did that positive feeling bring you?
- Make a list of possible advantages that the evolution you are resisting could bring you.
- Write or imagine a list of new people you might meet if you embrace that which you are struggling to accept.
- Considering all the ideas from previous points, write down some brief conclusions.

Chapter 6

HOW WE DO THINGS MATTERS

As you observe the team leaders around you and, hopefully, progress into positions of responsibility, you will see that the tasks themselves are of secondary importance and 'soft skills', such as leadership, analytical thinking, effective communication, emotional intelligence, etc, are essential.

When I finished university, I started working for one of the big four accountancy firms, within their graduate programme. Some of my peers had a brilliant academic record, came from the most prestigious universities and possessed many technical skills. Despite all this, their less job-specific abilities, such as people skills, were sadly lacking.

It is clear that in order to perform our roles well, it is essential to know the relevant technical subject matter and also possess the core skills necessary for the job. However, to enable us to function effectively at work - and in life - we also need to acquire and develop many skills which are not included in many traditional training programs.

Soft skills are capabilities or behaviours that we put into practice when we go about our daily lives. We could define them as our non-technical toolbox.

Everyone's list of desirable soft skills changes with time and culture, but in this section we will review some of those capabilities that are demanded by the market:

- Effective communication.
- Teamwork.
- Resilience.

We don't need to master all soft skills, but some are particularly necessary for positions of responsibility, while others are universal.

As usual, you will find exercises for you to self-enquire about your level of development in these skills. When you undertake them, you will be able to discover which ones make you shine and those which you may want to improve. Our own perception of our personalities and behaviour is not always the same as that of others. The closer both perceptions get, the more balanced we will be and the more objective we become.

In chapter 10 you will discover how we can deceive yourselves.

For this reason, I encourage you to send the exercises to a number of your colleagues and ask them to also score their perception of your behaviour in these areas.

EFFECTIVE COMMUNICATION

Communication is the basic tool we have for interacting with the world. Therefore, our communication skills make a massive difference to our interactions, to the impact we make and to our chances of success. Unfortunately, we often take risks with this success when using one-way communications, such as emails, reports or presentations.

Our ideas may be brilliant but if we are not able to communicate them effectively, we will fail to secure the attention and support of others.

We put our communication skills into practice in three areas, each having their particular attributes which we must take into account:

- Face-to-face interactions.
- Written messages.
- Presentations.

FACE-TO-FACE

Nowadays, and particularly in the post-COVID era, face-to-face encounters are becoming increasingly rare. In-person interactions give us the opportunity to build relationships and the trust that we talked about in the first part of this manual. Even if we have meetings by videoconference, we need to take care of some basic principles if we want to hold productive meetings which add value to those who take part. You can take care of your face-to-face communication with two basic requirements:

- Balancing the time you spend listening and speaking, and
- Paying full attention.

DO YOU HAVE BALANCED CONVERSATIONS?

Whether you're the type who hardly stops talking or if you find it hard to speak up, finding the right balance can make your communication more effective. Clearly, our ability to achieve this balance also depends on the people we communicate with but, by identifying which style we usually adopt, we can make an effort to strike a balance. Do be aware that it is very possible that our behaviour at home is different from our behaviour in the workplace. In my case, in personal situations I usually allow any loquacious people around me to continue their frequently lengthy discourses uninterrupted. In contrast, at work I have to make a conscious effort to stop talking occasionally and give others the opportunity to speak. A healthy balance is to take the initiative, gently putting the brakes on others when they get carried away by their unstoppable monologues, but also leaving free space for interruptions and comments when we find ourself monopolising the conversation.

How do you feel when you have a meeting with someone who clearly has their mind on something else?

If we take the time to be with someone, it's worth actively listening to them.

> 🔔 **WHEN WE LISTEN TO OTHERS, WE ARE ANALYSING THE INFORMATION THEY GIVE US WITH OUR ASSUMPTIONS, THOUGHTS, AND JUDGEMENTS.**

📝 In chapter 10 you will discover in what ways we can misrepresent.

The above distractions are a barrier to effective communication.

> 🔔 **WE CAN REDUCE THIS BIAS IF WE REALLY PAY ATTENTION TO WHAT WE ARE BEING TOLD.**

Being fully present is harder than it seems. We achieve it better by eliminating distractions, such as our mobile phones, the simultaneous use of applications or an open laptop screen.

Look the other person in the face and listen to what they say without automatically starting to prepare your answer. Check yourself when you listen to others: without realising it, you may be anticipating your response instead of actively listening to them. When meeting with more than one person or in a video conference, it is easy to become distracted by our ideas, thoughts and potential responses, making us effectively absent from the meeting and blocking the chance of effective communication.

Score from 1 to 10 the following statements, with 1 being "Completely false" and 10 "Completely true":

When I communicate face-to-face...

	Score
I pay my utmost attention to others when they speak	
I silence my mobile and close apps on my computer screen	
I find a way to be heard if others are monopolising the discussion	
I am aware of when I talk excessively	
I ensure that I leave space for others to speak	
I try to put aside my presumptions	
I listen to others without anticipating my response	

- For each response with a score greater than 7, write a specific example that demonstrates that behaviour in the past week.
- For each answer below a 5, write down a practical action you can take to foster this ability.
- You can send this exercise to colleagues and ask them to rate the statements regarding how they perceive your behaviour in this area.
- Write down what you have become aware of by carrying out this exercise.

WRITE WITH CARE

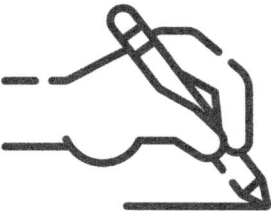

If I had one pound for every time I've misinterpreted a written message, I could afford a very good holiday – and if they had given me another pound every time I have been misunderstood, that holiday could be quite a long one.

We are bombarded with so much written information that it is understandable if we scan messages instead of reading them carefully. If we also bear in mind that what is written often lacks clear context, I am not surprised that we find ourselves in so many situations of confusion and disagreement.

This is complicated even further when communication is between people who do not share the same mother tongue.

I will share my tricks for reducing the emotional burden of messages in chapter 7.

In one of the projects I have supported as a consultant and mentor, the entrepreneur I accompanied had many problems with the team because of his written communication style. His messages landed like bombshells, creating confusion, frustration and general havoc. It was not rare to read messages from him such as, "This is useless for me," "You are doing your job badly," or "I want you to send it to me right now." From his point of view, he was being direct, because it was his way of trying to make the company reach its potential. The reality is that with this way of expressing himself, rather than providing solutions, he only managed to increase the tension and the number of resignations of his staff.

WHETHER YOU ARE RIGHT OR NOT IS IRRELEVANT – YOU ARE FAR MORE LIKELY TO ACHIEVE BETTER RESULTS IF YOU TAKE TIME TO REVIEW AND ADJUST YOUR WRITTEN COMMUNICATIONS.

Have you ever had a long chain of emails or chat messages that, instead of achieving anything, left a sea of confusion? To reduce the likelihood that our messages will be misinterpreted, we need to be cautious with the wording we tend to use without conscious thought. The interpretation of many expressions, the meaning of which we may take for granted, may be very differently construed by others.

There are times when conversations do not make progress because we do not leave a way clearly open for others to take the next step. In a written conversation, if we want to direct the conversation towards a particular point, it helps to leave a clear opportunity for our correspondent to make a further suggestion or comment.

For example, one of the professionals I have mentored was conducting part of the negotiation of her new contractual terms in writing. She asked me to take a look at her email before she sent it and give her my advice. She had clearly drafted the conditions she wanted but at no point did she suggest an alternative for the recipient, should any of the conditions be unacceptable. After our conversation, she added a clear but respectful way for the negotiation to continue, instead of forcing it to end with a 'yes' or a 'no'.

The last point to consider in written messages - and the most important, although it may seem obvious to you - is the following: BEWARE OF CONFLICT.

> ⚠ **MANY CONFLICT SITUATIONS BEGIN, OR WORSEN CONSIDERABLY, BECAUSE OF WRITTEN MESSAGES.**

Let's go back to the example of the entrepreneur I mentioned and his communication style. Impatience and lack of time led him to fight all his battles in writing, wreaking havoc around him. I am sure that you can think of times when, after receiving an email or message, you were hit by a hot flush throughout your body, turning your state of tranquility into worry, panic or anger.

Although we do not always have time to carefully prepare all written messages to people who are particularly important or ones sent to a person who we know needs to be dealt with sensitively, you can reflect, put yourself in the shoes of the other and ask yourself:

- What response do I want to encourage in that person?
- Am I making any accusations or complaints?
- Have I added anything that could be misinterpreted?
- Am I providing new information that may cause surprise?
- Would I feel comfortable if this message is shared?
- Is my language considerate?
- Are my statements objective or do they personalise?

The use of language is an art and if you pay attention to how you communicate in writing, you will see the beneficial impact it can have on your relationships as well as improving your communication skills.

Score from 1 to 10 the following statements, with 1 being "Completely false" and 10 "Completely true":

When I communicate in writing...

	Score
I am specific and include whatever context the other person may need	
I de-personalise the affirmations I make	
I am explicit about what I expect the other person to do	
I avoid addressing conflicting issues not previously discussed in person	
I propose alternative courses of action for the other party	

- For each response with a score greater than 7, write a concrete example that demonstrated that behaviour in the past week.
- For each answer below a 5, write a practical action you can take to foster this ability.
- You can send this exercise to colleagues and ask them to rate the statements regarding how they perceive your behaviour in this area.
- Write down what you have become aware of by carrying out this exercise.

CAPTIVATE YOUR AUDIENCE

People often refer to 'storytelling', which effectively means framing our messages as if we were telling people a story or anecdote, so ask yourself: am I able to deliver compelling messages which are memorable, capture the attention of others, and boost my influence at work? If the answer is "not enough", I have created the acronym "HUSSLE" to remind you how to take the necessary steps to improve your communication in presentations.

> [!] WE LIVE IN A WORLD OVERLOADED WITH INFORMATION, SO IT IS HARD TO GRAB OUR AUDIENCE'S ATTENTION.

> [!] HUSSLE IS AN EASY ACRONYM TO HELP YOU REMEMBER SIX IMPORTANT STEPS IN THIS STORYTELLING TECHNIQUE AND ENABLE YOU TO BUILD SOLID PRESENTATIONS.

HERO

Every good story has a hero or heroine, ideally one to whom we can relate. Set the scene by introducing the context of the circumstances and if possible, include elements that enable your audience to connect with your hero or situation.

Ask yourself: what are the similarities between my hero and the members of the audience? In a work environment, we may show similarities between departments or mention common challenges.

UPHILL STRUGGLE

Present the problem. Emotion is a powerful tool and introducing an obstacle which your hero needs to overcome is an excellent way to get your audience to empathise with them, using elements of sadness, frustration, happiness or humour.

Ask yourself: what are the negative consequences of the situation that has happened or could happen? How can this affect my audience?

SOLUTION

After presenting the problem, it is essential to present - or propose - a solution that lifts the mood of our story or presentation. Nobody likes to dwell too much on problems - we all like solutions, even when the end result is different from the solution we proposed at the beginning. This is the turning point that brings a touch of drama and directs the story towards a satisfactory resolution.

Ask yourself: how has the situation been resolved or how will it be resolved? What positive consequences can be drawn from the circumstances?

SHOW

Put on a good show using words that are memorable, use body language or examples that illustrate the situation or the characters who are part of the story. In a work context, this can be done using meaningful data and graphical information which enhances the argument you're trying to reinforce.

Ask yourself: how can I prove my arguments with a simple statement or a key piece of information?

LEARNING

All good stories bring learning and food for thought, especially if that learning can also be used by others. For example, in a work context, it's beneficial to explain what changes you've made or have planned, to avoid encountering the same obstacles in the future.

Ask yourself: what would I do differently the next time? What processes or controls can be implemented?

EXTRAORDINARY

Sparking your audience's imagination can be a wonderful tool to reinforce their memory of you, personally, and of your presentation. Use metaphors, visual images, and acronyms to make your presentation easy to remember and memorable. In this step, HUSSLE has played that important role.

Ask yourself: how can I bring memorable images into my story?

Storytelling techniques help messages and presentations gain depth and enable us to connect with the audience, making our presentations more interesting and memorable.

If you'd like an example of this technique, you will find it in the final chapter, but don't read it just yet.

Think about a presentation or proposal that you have recently carried out and give a score from 1 to 10 depending on the presence and relevance of the different elements of HUSSLE, 1 being "Completely absent" and 10 "Completely included":

	Score
Hero	
Uphill struggle	
Solution	
Show	
Learning	
Extraordinary	

- For those items with a score below 7, write down how you could have improved it.

TEAMWORK

Interaction with others is inevitable in the vast majority of situations. If you try to think of a job that is entirely solitary, it's practically impossible. Even a goatherd has to go to the market occasionally!

The capacity to successfully work with a team, a skill demanded nowadays by almost every company, is also the key to enable us to make our day-to-day work experience more enjoyable and achieve better results.

> [!] TEAMWORK INVOLVES BEING ASSERTIVE IN OUR INTERACTIONS WITH OTHERS BUT AT THE SAME TIME ALLOWING THEM TO PLAY THEIR OWN ROLES.

Effective teamwork can lead to many advantages: adding value, being self-critical, and advancing mutual benefits or goals for the group.

The practicalities about the way in which that is managed include the definition of roles and the distribution of tasks, etc. That's the easy part! However, to put this ability into practice, attitude and behaviours are important, as is the culture of the organisation and the people around us. We can't work well in groups if others don't do their part, but our behaviour can make all the difference so that the balance is tipped in favour of team collaboration.

In real life, I have observed how this is one of the great challenges facing most organisations. Conflicts of interest between people or departments are common, which makes it much more difficult to carry out their designated functions. Sometimes, to be able to work in a team, we need to lose something at an individual level, and that is regrettable. Also, when colleagues fail to do their part, it is easy to inadvertently create friction or resentment.

When asked if we are able to work as a team, the automatic answer is usually 'yes' but we should be honest with ourselves and assess how developed this capacity really is, so let's consider it

Score from 1 to 10 the following statements, with 1 being "Completely false" and 10 "Completely true":

When I work as part of a team...

	Score
I encourage others to provide their opinions	
When I disagree with others, I try to understand their points of view	
I listen as much as I speak	
I change my point of view often	
I pursue goals that benefit all parties	
I like to lead	
I like it when others take the lead	
I take the initiative so that we all know who has to do what	
I pursue team objectives above my own needs or those of my department	
When a team member does not pull their weight, I look for solutions collaboratively	

- For each response with a score greater than 7, write a concrete example that demonstrates that behaviour that in the past week.
- For answers below a 5, write a practical action you can take to foster this ability.
- You can send this exercise to peers and ask them to rate the affirmations regarding how they perceive your behaviour in this area.
- Write what you have become aware of by carrying out this exercise.

RESILIENCE

Having resilience means not throwing in the towel no matter what challenges are encountered, persisting and recovering, and then even undertaking further projects.

> ⚠ RESILIENCE IS ABOUT BEING ABLE TO OVERCOME FAILURES OR ADAPT TO CHANGES IN OUR LIVES.

This skill is particularly important if we are to move on to new areas of responsibility.

> ⚠ WE ENHANCE OUR RESILIENCE WITH FOUR CHARACTERISTICS: ADAPTABILITY, REFLECTION, POSITIVE ATTITUDE AND RESPONSIBILITY.

We can shorten the agony and recover quickly from failures if we face the situation as soon as it arises, being proactive and tying up loose ends.

It is natural that our internal dialogue becomes a source of negative thoughts on occasions when we fail or make mistakes. Although we must avoid getting overwhelmed by those negative thoughts, it is important to reflect on the events rather than continuing as if nothing had happened or burying our heads in the sand. Constructive reflection can lead us to learning opportunities and seeing such experiences from new perspectives. There are two simple questions we can ask to help us to turn failures into development opportunities.

- What could I do differently to get a better result next time?
- How do I turn that into a new attitude or behaviour for the future?

Positive attitude — This is considered a soft skill in itself. If we are able to find a plus side or a learning opportunity, we can transform that difficult scenario into an asset for the future. Furthermore, resilience is linked to our level of self-esteem and strengthens our belief in our own capabilities.

Responsibility — We must take our share of responsibility for failures. However, it is also important to keep an open mind and understand the perspectives of others, even in situations where the fault apparently lies with someone else or with the working environment itself.

Instead of simply getting back onto our feet every time we stumble over an obstacle, we can learn to avoid them when they appear along the road. As Confucius said: "Our greatest glory is not in never falling, but rising every time we fall."

Score from 1 to 10 the following statements, with 1 being "Completely false" and 10 "Completely true":

When I make a mistake or fail ...

	Score
I recognise my share of responsibility in generating the outcome	
I don't always blame others for a negative result	
I identify what I can do in the future to avoid a similar outcome	
I don't spend an excessive amount of time dwelling on it	
I maintain a positive attitude	
I take preventative measures when possible	
It doesn't take me long to recover emotionally	
I tie up loose ends or pending matters swiftly	
My reaction is always to look for solutions	

- For each response with a score greater than 7, write a concrete example that demonstrates that behaviour that in the past week.
- For each answer below a 5, write a practical action you can take to foster this ability.
- You can send this exercise to colleagues and ask them to rate the affirmations regarding how they perceive your behaviour in this area.
- Write down what you have become aware of by doing out this exercise.

There are many other soft skills, some companies creating their own list of skills and fostering them in their teams. We have explored some of them in this chapter but the list could be endless, so a basic exercise you can carry out to define and promote any soft skill would be as follows:

- What elements characterise this soft skill?
- What behaviours demonstrate such elements in practice?
- Think of specific examples that demonstrate such behaviours.
- Seek the opinion of others to corroborate your perception.

Below is a list of the most sought-after soft skills, which you may be interested to research individually and evaluate your level of development about them.

Assertiveness	Leadership
Problem solving	Empathy
Tolerance to pressure	Constant learning
Analytical mindset	Critical thinking
Adaptability	Sociability
Proactivity	Customer mindset
Honesty and professional ethics	Organization and planning
Growth mindset	Attention to detail
Innovation	Punctuality
Perseverance	Initiative

Chapter 7

HOW OTHERS SEE YOU

We have talked about soft skills; how important they are and how they can make all the difference to our professional performance. To improve in all of them, to learn and progress, the single and crucial tool we have at our disposal is the ability to understand, use and promote feedback. That is what we will talk about in this chapter.

I started work for one company during a rather turbulent time for my department and as my line manager was overwhelmed, I didn't get the chance to forge a strong relationship with her. During my first three months we had very few opportunities to meet on a one-to-one basis but one evening we both attended an office function. We found ourselves standing next to each other at the bar in the crowded venue and tried to converse over the loud music and the general chatter. For some strange reason, she decided to use this opportunity to give me feedback on my progress. I am well aware that everyone tends to be selective with what we remember and I imagine that she must have also said something positive, but all I heard was a diatribe on my failings being broadcast in public. I was dumbfounded and, as soon as I could, I ended the conversation and left to catch my train, utterly

devastated and feeling as if the ground was shaking under my feet. That conversation was the beginning of an unstoppable deterioration in our relationship and even now, after many years, I find it hard to believe that she had so little sensitivity.

To explore this topic, let's:

- Demystify some ideas.
- Provide feedback considerately.
- Make the most of other people's opinions.
- Take some tools home.

LET'S DEMYSTIFY FEEDBACK

Feedback is a topic that can give rise to much debate. Some companies boast of having a culture of feedback and, if their policies promote 360-degree feedback, they are quick to boast that they lead the way in this regard. I can honestly say that throughout all the years of my professional career, I have often observed that this is a misunderstood and misused area. Many companies think that running a training course for a few hours prepares team leaders to develop the sensitivity and experience that is required to do this well or, which is worse, many companies don't even provide such training, hence we learn through the examples of our superiors, both good and bad.

Organisational culture also has a great deal of impact. I have worked with many companies where a performance evaluation is deemed to have taken place when a line manager has informed their team of their opinion on whether or not they have done a good job.

⎡!⎤ GOOD FEEDBACK GOES FAR BEYOND THE TASKS OF THE ROLE AND, IF IT IS RELATED TO THE INDIVIDUAL'S SOFT SKILLS, IT CAN HAVE A LOT OF IMPACT ON THEIR PERSONAL AND PROFESSIONAL PROGRESSION.

Many of us have been left wondering why we were not chosen for promotion when we were confident of having done our job perfectly. I remember a time when I felt cheated and frustrated because a colleague, whose performance, in my opinion, was worse than mine, got the promotion that I wanted. Does that sound familiar? Well, the truth is that even when the tasks themselves are perfectly executed, without the required accompanying soft skills it is difficult to progress.

Thinking that feedback is only necessary in a downwards direction in the chain of command is a mistake and is also a loss of opportunity. Team leaders need to know their team's opinions if they wish to improve themselves, even when they feel reluctant to do so, in order to gain a better understanding of their team's needs and to be more effective in their roles.

Peer-to-peer feedback can also play an important role, as they provide complementary insights to what our managers or teams perceive.

> ⓘ SEEKING OPINIONS FROM ALL DIRECTIONS IS WORTH THE EFFORT, SINCE EACH TYPE OF RELATIONSHIP CAN SHED LIGHT ON DIFFERENT PERSPECTIVES, THUS MAKING OUR OVERALL IMPRESSION MORE BALANCED.

I have had many opportunities to give and receive feedback, experiencing the consequences first hand. I have been grateful for constructive opinions that were expressed sensitively, but distressed when criticism was tactless, blunt or dropped like a bombshell in public.

Feedback can be a great gift if it is carefully thought out and delivered. It can also be like a body-blow which causes hurt, leaving the recipient in real distress - sometimes with irreparable consequences.

> ⓘ APPROACHING EVALUATIONS, GIVEN OR RECEIVED, WITH SENSITIVITY AND CARE CAN LEAD TO EXCELLENT RESULTS.

We can enhance our team's performance if we are effective when providing assessments, giving them the motivation and confidence to seek advancement in their careers.

If we are willing to listen and accept the opinions of others, it is easy to improve our performance. We get closer to our colleagues, building trust with them and, above all, come to understand how they perceive us. This last point is a crucial area for development at a personal and professional level. For many years, it was my custom to invite all the people with whom I interacted regularly to give me their candid opinions on my performance and that of my team. They included team members, bosses, reception staff and people from other departments – both senior and junior. Of course, not everyone wished to participate but, by inviting their comments, I made it clear that I actively sought and valued their opinions. From these assessments I learned a lot and also created bonds of trust across the organisation.

Good feedback is balanced because it includes both praise for strengths and suggestions for improvement.

WE OFTEN AVOID GIVING CONSTRUCTIVE CRITICISM BECAUSE WE DO NOT FEEL COMFORTABLE DOING SO, OR WORRY ABOUT HURTING THE OTHER PERSON'S FEELINGS AND DAMAGING THE RELATIONSHIP.

I have encountered many people who were happy to complain about their subordinates or colleagues but were unable or unwilling to openly address areas of improvement with them and, at the other end of the spectrum, people who readily and openly expressed opinions but chose the most inappropriate times or places to do so. However, if we do not receive any kind of comment or assessment at all, this can lead us to feel insecure or anxious in our jobs.

⚠ IF WE ARE INCAPABLE OF GIVING CONSTRUCTIVE ASSESSMENTS TO A TEAM FOR WHOM WE ARE RESPONSIBLE, WE ARE NOT DOING A GOOD JOB AS A MANAGER AND WE ARE ALSO FAILING THEM AT A HUMAN LEVEL.

Feedback is not only an opportunity to improve the performances around us, but also a great motivational tool for us to appreciate and celebrate the successful and positive attitudes we observe. Good, constructive feedback, makes people feel important and valued – something everyone appreciates.

PROVIDE FEEDBACK WITH SENSITIVITY

In organisations where appraisals take place, performance ratings are often associated with year-end evaluations. However, continual feedback is an inevitable occurrence in our day to day lives, whether we like it or not.

⚠ WE ARE CONSTANTLY GIVING FEEDBACK TO OTHERS, OFTEN WITHOUT REALISING IT, SO IT IS IMPORTANT TO BE AWARE OF THIS AND CAREFUL WHEN WE CHOOSE OUR WORDS.

It can easily be that a casual, passing comment made to a colleague may be received as a judgement without our even being aware of it. If it is well delivered and received it will be positive for the relationship but, if not, it has the potential to cause harm. I'm not suggesting that we go around the office wrapping every comment we make in cottonwool, but we should be aware of the power of our words and the impact they can have, depending on how they are received.

Choosing our language carefully, not only when we're preparing well-intentioned feedback, is beneficial. For example, if someone hands us a report or a draft presentation, saying, "Let's go over this together to see if we can improve it," is better than saying, "This needs to be fixed," or, "It's wrong." There are small subtleties in the way we communicate which have a significant impact on those around us. Here are my two recommendations to mitigate the risk of unintentionally creating offence:

1. Avoid personalising. For example, instead of saying, "Your presentation," or, "What you have prepared," say, "The presentation," or, "The draft." This will reduce the likelihood that the other person will take your comments as a personal attack.
2. Speak positively. Instead of saying, "This is wrong," or, "It's not worth it," you can say, "We can improve it," "It could be more effective if ..." This may seem obvious but, if you pay attention to what you say to others – and what others say to you - you will notice that there are usually opportunities for improvement in this regard.

⚠ YOU CAN REDUCE THE RISK OF UNINTENTIONALLY OFFENDING OTHERS BY MAKING POSITIVE STATEMENTS AND AVOIDING PERSONALISING.

These tips can be applicable to any area of life - not only when we give feedback at work. If you want to check it out, pay attention to how others express themselves when they are making any sort of complaint. I remember one day when I was at an airport and all the morning flights were cancelled because of the weather. I was at the customer service queue and a disgruntled passenger was complaining vociferously to the check-in clerk as if she had personally organised the fog. The clerk was attempting to deal with this very difficult situation in a professional way, but was understandably losing interest in helping that angry and unreasonable man find a place on an alternative flight. Although this may seem an exaggerated example, the truth is that we are frequently unaware of how we express ourselves and the impact that our words can have on the emotional state of others and their desire to support or help us.

PREPARATION

As in conflict management, the preparation phase of our assessment is very important. When we improvise, it is possible that key aspects can be accidentally omitted. When we plan the conversation, we can make sure that ideas that are truly important will be discussed. It also helps us to balance feedback because we can take care to include both praise and development points.

Make sure there are more positives points than negative ones. There are sources that recommend at least six positive points for each negative, although this is not always practical and can even sound somewhat forced.

> ⚠️ IT IS IMPORTANT TO PREPARE OUR COMMENTS FROM A POSITIVE VIEWPOINT AND WITH A GENUINE INTENTION OF WANTING TO ADD VALUE TO THE PERSON WHO IS GOING TO RECEIVE IT; NOT TO GIVE A REPRIMAND OR MAKE A REPROACH.

When preparing feedback, try to include aspects relating to two areas: the work itself and soft skills or behaviours. Instead of preparing an endless list of points, try to group your observations into generic topics from a solutions approach and avoid presenting them as problems.

For example, if a person is usually late with their tasks. Instead of saying, "You handed in several deliverables late," we can say, "Changing the way you prioritise your to-do list could help you deliver things on time more often." Or if someone is a little abrupt with colleagues or clients, we could say, "Your communication style might be perceived as 'direct' which could make some people less inclined to listen." Support your claims with concrete examples of situations that have occurred instead of sticking to generic phrases, for example, "During the meeting with ..." or, "In project X ...".

It is advisable to let the person know that you want to have a feedback conversation, thus giving them the opportunity to prepare themselves.

If feedback is not something that is discussed openly in your workplace, you can simply ask people to meet you in order to 'discuss' specific topics or to 'ask for their support' with something. This type of neutral language helps to start conversations implying that we wish to convey our opinion, to assist them, or to ask that they do something differently in order to help us.

It is not necessary to refer to such a meeting as 'feedback'. Calling it a 'conversation' when thanks or congratulations are offered and/or ideas are shared regarding ways in which some aspects may be improved, is effectively the same thing.

DELIVERY

> ⚠ **START THE CONVERSATION BY INVITING THE OTHER PERSON TO GIVE YOU THEIR OPINION ON HOW THE SITUATION, TOPIC OR EVALUATION PERIOD HAS PROGRESSED.**

Keep an open mind and consider what they say in order to adapt the comments you have prepared, taking into account any new information that appears during the conversation. Occasionally, new information or ideas arise during the meeting that we had not taken into account and which are important for your assessment to be balanced.

When we share what we'd like the other person to change in their behaviour, it is important to be understanding about any possible reasons for it, of which we may be unaware; for example, someone might be regularly late because they have problems with their child's daycare. It also helps when we articulate what advantages may follow from the change that we propose.

These conversations should not have a winner or a loser; ideally both parties will find it useful and learn something in the process.

> ⚠ **END THE CONVERSATION BY ENCOURAGING THE PERSON RECEIVING THE FEEDBACK TO SUMMARISE KEY MESSAGES, THUS ENSURING THAT WHAT THEY TAKE AWAY FROM YOU INCLUDES BOTH PRAISE AND AREAS FOR IMPROVEMENT.**

If our comments are not well received there is a risk that people will ignore the positive and leave the meeting only with the negative — or vice versa. That is not the purpose of such a conversation, so always try to make sure that the message has been received in a balanced way – including both the positive and the negative.

Praise in writing is beneficial but when feedback includes areas for improvement, it is advisable to avoid email or other written formats so that the message does not become a unilateral communication, taken out of context.

Depending on the circumstances and the specific corporate culture, it may be appropriate to follow up by sending a hard copy of the full assessment. The likelihood that written feedback will cause friction or offence is lower once contextualized by having had a conversation previously.

DO NOT LEAVE ANYTHING UNSAID

Having to dismiss anyone from the company or organisation frequently provokes anger and confusion, due to this coming as a complete shock to the unfortunate employee when no previous warnings or indications have been given. It is not fair to fire someone if we have not made an effort to make them aware of our concerns, ensuring that they understand which aspects of their performance are unacceptable and giving them the opportunity to rectify them.

When we provide feedback about immediate changes required if the recipient is to bring their performance up to an adequate standard, it is advisable to give it in writing as well as verbally, to support any possible future disciplinary process.

MAKE THE MOST OTHER PEOPLE'S OPINIONS

To avoid repeating some of the messages that we have discussed in previous chapters, here is a gentle reminder about the two steps that are most important when you are in the position of receiving feedback instead of giving it: preparation and listening.

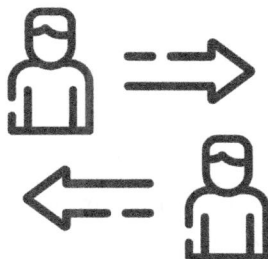

Feedback sessions are also an opportunity to express to others what you think and how they can help you.

Many people are lazy when it comes to preparing their appraisal meetings and yes, it can be tedious. However, setting any reluctance aside is the only way one can, at least partly, take control of the situation and not become a mere observer in the process.

If you're in an organisation where appraisals aren't the norm, you're likely to receive many reviews informally, even if they're not always balanced or delivered sensitively. If that is the case, you can still be proactive with your development and ask your manager and the people around you to contribute to your growth by sharing their views. You may not have the ability to change the culture of a company single-handed, but it's possible to start influencing that culture through your own actions. If enough people follow the example you set, you may ultimately see the desired changes being implemented.

A natural reaction when given constructive feedback, especially when we are not expecting it, is to become defensive. As we will see in chapter 10, what others say and what we hear is not necessarily the same and so when we first hear negative comments, our perception may not be completely objective. When we disagree with someone's view, we may feel perturbed.

> 🗨️ CALM DOWN, REFLECT ON WHAT WAS ACTUALLY SAID AND THEN TAKE SOME TIME TO CONSIDER IT OBJECTIVELY.

> 🗨️ EVEN IF THE FEEDBACK IS NOT TOTALLY ACCURATE, THERE IS ALWAYS THE OPPORTUNITY TO LEARN SOMETHING FROM IT.

Looking back on evaluations that have been given to me in the past; the ones which hurt me the most at the time were also the ones that contributed the most to my development. They helped me notice things that I was not aware of, and prompted me to adapt my style and behaviour in order to get better results. I remember attending a meeting which I thought I had handled well and in which I had defended my opinion passionately. Afterwards, my manager told me that I had not really listened to the divisional director we were talking with, my style had been too direct and I had sounded obstinate. I was stunned! Not only did he not appreciate my passion but he viewed me as being stubborn (my words, not his). Although I needed some time to digest all this, I came to realise that he was right and that while my natural passion can be an asset, I also needed to temper it if I wanted to make the most of the situations I encounter and gain the support of others.

In cases of doubt and to avoid misunderstandings, ask questions which you consider appropriate during the conversation. We tend to stick to our initial interpretation of other people's words and this means, from time to time, that we cling to that first impression. If we take the time to investigate a little more in some aspects by communicating with each other, we can better understand what they mean and digest the information accurately.

Be cautious, as our minds often betray us by holding on to some messages while ignoring others.

If you receive feedback that includes aspects which surprise you, one option is to ask the other person to give you some time to think about it and if you might continue the conversation at a later date. This will give you the opportunity to digest the information, think about what you could change and formulate an appropriate, constructive response.

DIGEST AND ACT

Receiving compliments is usually pleasant, even though it can sometimes be difficult for us to accept them. Enjoy them and congratulate yourself on what you do well, without becoming arrogant. We have a tendency to focus solely on either the positive or the negative but, as we do when we prepare feedback for others, we need to remember that being balanced with ourselves enables us to digest the information given to us in a healthy way.

Once the key points are digested, it is good to think about how we may put into action any required improvements. Sometimes we can seek out additional training or support, while some of us will need to change our mindset or behaviour. Considering practical and viable ways to take action in these areas of development is important for our evolution.

⚠ IF WE DON'T TURN FEEDBACK INTO ACTION, IT WON'T HAVE THE TRANSFORMATIVE IMPACT IT IS CAPABLE OF GENERATING.

Performance appraisal meetings can be either a nightmare for both parties or a pleasurable experience that strengthens the bond between manager and team member – or a mixture of both. If possible, having this conversation in an informal setting is beneficial; over a coffee or by having lunch together. Giving appraisal meetings an air of positivity or a sense of occasion, lifts the atmosphere from a cold, routine meeting.

⚠ THE ABSENCE OF SURPRISES IS A GOOD SIGN. DIALOGUE AND COMMUNICATION BETWEEN TEAM MEMBERS AND THEIR MANAGER THROUGHOUT THE YEAR IS THE BASIS FOR GOOD RELATIONSHIPS.

The exchange of opinions and feedback happens every day, so the evaluation meeting should be a time and space for validating information given previously, not an opportunity to spring surprises on issues that have not been properly managed on a day-to-day basis.

⚠ ALLOW THE CONVERSATION TO COME TO A NATURAL CLOSE, ALWAYS ENDING IT ON A POSITIVE NOTE.

Often this is the only opportunity for two people to have a conversation focused only on the development of them both, which in itself can be an opportunity to strengthen the relationship.

Think of a time when you received feedback that caused you discomfort or distress:

- Summarise that negative feeling in a short sentence.
- Describe what aspects you perceived as negative and why.
- Review the original summary phrase and change the words, if necessary, to express it neutrally and without personalising.

- Write down what positive intention the person who gave you that feedback had.
- Describe what you learned from this assessment at the time or could learn in the future.
- Write down what you've become aware of by doing this exercise.

Think of a situation where you gave feedback that caused discomfort or distress:

- Summarise that negative feeling in a short sentence.
- Describe what aspects you think were perceived as negative and why. Review the original summary phrase and change the words, if necessary, to express it neutrally and without personalising.
- Write down what positive intention you had which you were unable to transmit.
- What could you have done differently to make that constructive criticism better received?
- Write down what you've become aware of by doing this exercise.

Think of a situation where you received feedback that pleased you:

- Summarise that positive assessment in a short sentence.
- Describe what aspects you perceived as positive and why.
- Review the original summary phrase and change the words, if necessary, to express it neutrally and without personalising.
- Write down what positive intention the person who gave you that feedback had.
- Describe what learning about their feelings brought you, or can bring you.
- Write down what you've become aware of by doing this exercise.

TAKE SOME WORK-TOOLS HOME WITH YOU

Feedback also happens in the home. Bringing into our private lives some of our skills regarding the delivering of assessments can have many benefits.

At home, we make positive comments all the time - we say, "I love you," to each other, we say how wonderful they are, and that's fantastic. Let's keep doing it!

That said, we are not always tactful but clear; or forthright and effective when it comes to giving constructive feedback in our private environments. We tend to either avoid expressing ourselves at all or go overboard about what we do not like.

> [!] NEGATIVE FEEDBACK, POORLY MANAGED, CREATES FRICTION AND RESENTMENT UNTIL ONE DAY WE SUDDENLY GO OFF AT THE DEEP END OR, EVEN WORSE, THE RELATIONSHIP DETERIORATES SO FAR THAT RECOVERY IS DIFFICULT, IF NOT IMPOSSIBLE.

For this reason, I suggest that we should also try to be more professional in how we manage personal relationships and, as far as possible and is appropriate, readily offer and accept feedback in them.

I'm not suggesting that we should have evaluation meetings with our children, husbands, wives, parents or siblings. That's obviously not feasible or desirable in a family setting!

> [!] WE CAN LOOK FOR MOMENTS TO COMMUNICATE, WITH RESPECT AND AFFECTION TO OTHERS, WHAT CREATES DIFFICULTIES FOR US.

If we need help or we feel that someone close to us is harming, disrespecting or making us feel uncomfortable in some way, we need to effectively communicate that to them.

An interesting exercise may be to choose a relationship that is important to you - one in which you feel there is something negative, destructive, or that causes you harm - and apply the same approach as in the previous sections. Make a list, try to think about what aspects can be improved, how to group those messages or areas of development and look for the opportunity to communicate those ideas.

⚠ SHARE YOUR THOUGHTS CALMLY WHEN YOU HAVE THE OPPORTUNITY TO DO SO, AND WHEN THERE IS NO ATMOSPHERE OF CONFRONTATION. AVOID EXPLAINING YOURSELF BY TELLING THEM WHAT THEY ARE DOING WRONG, BUT RATHER BY STATING HOW YOU FEEL AND HOW THEY MAY BE ABLE TO SUPPORT YOU.

See the impact this can have on your relationships:

⚠ IF WE CAN JETTISON THE MANY CAUSES OF ANNOYANCE THAT WE OFTEN ALLOW TO BUILD UP AND CARRY AROUND WITH US IN OUR PRIVATE RELATIONSHIPS, LET THEM GO NATURALLY, WITHOUT AGGRESSION AND AS SOON AS WE BECOME AWARE OF THEM, WE CAN HAVE HEALTHIER, LONGER LASTING AND MORE HONEST CONNECTIONS.

When we identify how our words and actions affect others in a non-positive way, we can make changes and strengthen our relationships.

Think of a time when you expressed your opinion at home and it was not well received:

- Summarise that negative feedback in a short sentence.
- Describe what aspects you think were perceived as negative and why.
- Review the original summary phrase and change the words, if necessary, to express it neutrally and without personalising.
- Write down what positive intention you had and were unable to convey.
- What could you have done differently to make that constructive criticism better received?
- Write down what you've acknowledged and/or learnt by doing this exercise.

Chapter 8

FAILURE IS NOT WHAT IT SEEMS

Not long ago I was embroiled in a tense meeting with a client, one of several we had had in a matter of weeks. The atmosphere could have been cut with a knife. He was restless and impatient; his comments were curt and becoming louder as the meeting progressed. Eventually, he raised his voice even further and demanded to know why we had not finished his project weeks ago. I was already tired of offering explanations and did not know what more I could say to re-establish our previously good communication, which had somehow broken down several weeks earlier. For some obscure reason, he repeatedly asked me the same question – one which I had tried to answer many times but which he failed to accept. It rapidly became obvious that both the question and the answer were irrelevant. The underlying truth was that our relationship was broken. He had lost his patience and, with it, his confidence in me. Once I realised this, I finally said, "If this isn't good enough and you're not happy with my performance, that's okay, I'll just leave."

Wow! There I was at the age of 48, with a lot of experience and value to offer this project but, for the first time in my career I was, in effect, being fired.

As much as it hurt my pride, I had done the best I could and accepting that this cycle was over was

the most sensible thing I could do. This is a lesson I learned a long time ago from my many failures; hence, failure is the subject of this chapter.

⚠️ ACCEPTING AND DIGESTING FAILURE PROPERLY IS ONE OF THE BEST SKILLS WE CAN BUILD DURING OUR PERSONAL AND PROFESSIONAL DEVELOPMENT JOURNEY.

We will therefore go over some basic principles.

DON'T TURN A BLIND EYE – OR A DEAF EAR

I recently saw a video of the writer and lecturer, Sergi Torres, where he talked about crisis. He made a striking observation that illustrates this concept well. Translated roughly from the Spanish, he said that a crisis is not something that happens but is simply the manifestation of things that were hidden outside our area of consciousness, but which are now becoming evident.

⚠️ OUR INABILITY TO RECOGNISE THAT A RELATIONSHIP OR SOMETHING SIMILAR HAS COME TO AN END, IS EXACTLY WHAT PREVENTS US FROM SEEKING BETTER ALTERNATIVES AND ENJOYING SUCCESS IN A NEW SCENARIO.

There are plenty of reasons why we choose to look the other way or turn a blind eye to something. In fact, denial is generally recognised as the first stage of change. Perhaps we do not like to acknowledge that reality is not as we would wish it to be, or our egos are not allowing us to see the facts objectively. It may also be that we are afraid of change, consciously or not, and choose to stay hidden in our comfort zone.

⚠️ WHEN SOMETHING IS NOT RIGHT, THERE ARE SIGNS AROUND US THAT WE CAN DETECT.

Common signs to look out for are that conversations are tense, jobs are not delivered, questions arise which are difficult to answer, and frustration is a constant companion during the day.

One of the best steps I have taken was deciding to sell the business I founded - a tax and accountancy firm. I came to realise that I was never going to make a healthy profit if I wanted to maintain the quality standards I pursued. It was hard to say goodbye to being my own boss and accept that reality and what I wanted were two entirely different things. Continuing to pretend that I could achieve the unattainable was deceiving myself. In fact, I also observed the same self-deception in some of our clients, who had invested a lot of money in a business project but which simply did not have the necessary components to succeed. We often focus on what we want to see and not on the real picture. Why do we do this? The simple answer is because sometimes we get obsessed with pursuing our dreams, seeing situations solely from our own point of view at the cost of ignoring facts or signs which, if honestly considered, radically change our view of the landscape.

ACCEPT THAT IT IS OVER

Knowing when to throw in the towel is challenging but it is definitely a skill worth fostering. On the other hand, perseverance is key, even in the face of adversity, if we are to overcome obstacles and reach our goals.

> 〔!〕 IT IS ABOUT FINDING THE BALANCE BETWEEN WHEN TO GIVE UP AND WHEN (AND TO WHAT EXTENT) TO STRIVE TO FIND A WAY FORWARD.

Detecting the moment when you are sure that you have done all you can, but are equally sure that this is the right time to accept that it is over, is difficult but necessary. It is easier for us to see the inability of others to recognise such a moment than it is for ourselves. Maybe, as you read these words, someone you've encountered comes to mind who has failed to understand and accept the end of something they cared a great deal about. However, realistically, none of us manages to totally avoid that natural behaviour.

Returning to the example of my company, it is possible that people around me had already seen the signs before I did, and before I was ready to finally take the necessary step and call it quits. As good as the opportunity was, it wasn't for me.

At a personal level, when we finally pressed the 'Armageddon button' (as my estranged husband and I called it) when we decided to separate, we now realise and recognise that we had both known deep down about our differences and issues for a long time.

Resistance in accepting that a cycle in our life is over is the biggest barrier to ending suffering, moving on to take the next steps and being open to uncertainty. The moment we surrender, we suddenly feel a profound sense of relief.

WHAT CAN YOU LEARN?

Not everything that happens to us turns out to be positive and trying to force ourselves to stubbornly maintain a positive attitude is not faithful to our feelings. However, if we only ever act on our feelings and do not evaluate failures objectively, it is possible to get caught up in a cycle of repeating the same failure.

Einstein said, "Insanity is doing the same thing over and over again and expecting different results."

> OUR ABILITY TO LEARN FROM OUR EXPERIENCES, EVEN IN THE DEEPEST OF FAILURES, AND MODIFY OUR BEHAVIOUR ACCORDINGLY IS DIRECTLY RELATED TO SUCCESS.

It's always tempting to start pointing the finger at others or blaming external factors when we fail. However, even if some of those reasons are correct, placing the blame on them is absolutely useless because they are outside of our control.

> ⚠️ **TO IDENTIFY LEARNING OPPORTUNITIES, IT IS ESSENTIAL THAT WE LOOK AT THE EXPERIENCE OBJECTIVELY.**

The real question is: what could I have done differently?

> ⚠️ **TRULY VALUABLE LESSONS ARE THOSE THAT ARE DIRECTLY CONNECTED TO OUR OWN ACTIONS AND DECISIONS.**

MOVE ON (REALLY)

Failure inevitably gives way to pain, regret, and other uncomfortable emotions. It is important to feel these emotions and acknowledge them, as burying them will merely hide them deep within ourselves, causing damage which we may not notice immediately. When we fail, we must grieve and allow ourselves whatever time and space we need to feel that pain, as this is what helps us to heal. However, this does not mean that we should wallow in that pain forever.

It is important that you learn how to become aware of your repetitive or negative thoughts about the failure and stop them. We usually tell ourselves that we have got over it when, in fact, we have not. Our self-talk is the symptom. If you think about it too much, even if it's to tell yourself that you've turned the page, then you probably haven't got over it yet.

A curious twist in the example of failure with which I began this chapter, is that failure does not always mean the complete lack of a successful outcome. The dissatisfied client I mentioned actually contacted me several months later, having had time to reconsider and review what had happened from a broader perspective. He had acknowledged to himself that his frustration had come not only from my performance, but was also due to his own failure to manage such a tricky situation properly. We ultimately resumed our professional relationship from a renewed and more balanced perspective for both of us.

> ⚠ **THANKS TO OUR FAILURES, WE CAN BECOME REALLY SUCCESSFUL AT SOME THINGS AND ACHIEVE EXTRAORDINARY THINGS BUILT FROM PAST LEARNINGS.**

Think of someone in your life who is unable to give up, despite the evidence indicating that they should:

- Write a brief summary of the situation.
- Write down the advice you would give that person to help them see that they have done everything they can, to see the truth more clearly and encourage them to give up.
- Now think of a situation where you are the one who is going nowhere and give yourself the same advice, as you have written it, simply by changing their name to yours.

Think of a significant failure in your life:

- Describe that failure in a few words.
- Think of something you value today within the same environment (e.g., work, partner, family).
- Write automatically, without thinking too much, how that which you value now can be directly linked to the failure you thought about.
- Make a list of the things you learned during the experience that ended in failure.
- Write down what you did, or could do differently with your updated knowledge in mind.
- Write down any other thoughts that come to mind.

Part two

YOUR INNER WORLD

In this second part we will leave the outside world behind and travel within ourselves, in two sections:

Self: getting to know yourself better and acknowledge your experience as a possible interpretation among many others. That way you will begin to make choices more consciously and look at yourself in the mirror.

Well-being: connecting with your emotions and getting up close and personal with the characters of your ego. This will empower you to make decisions that are coherent with your needs and take care of your health.

SELF

Knowing yourself in more depth and becoming aware of how you are perceived is an essential step towards improving and reaching what you seek.

Chapter 9

GET TO KNOW YOURSELF

Thus far, we have explored the most important ways in which we can manage our external environment; issues that are commonly apparent in the workplace. In the second part of this manual, the main theme will be you - as a person and as a human being: individual, bright, vulnerable, exceptional, irrational and any other adjective that may describe you.

We are all unique and exceptional, while inherently equal to those around us. The fundamental question that motivated me to embark upon this project is this: what is the point of reaching our goals and being successful if we betray ourselves on the way towards achieving it? This question has many variants:

- What good is it to have recognition if I don't have time to enjoy life?
- What good does it do me if I make a lot of money but I sleep badly due to stress?
- What is the point of getting the next promotion in the career ladder if I am not enthusiastic about it?
- What's the point of working on a project if I don't believe in it?

⚠ REGARDLESS OF THE ANSWER, IT IS IMPORTANT THAT OUR ACTIONS ARE CONSISTENT WITH WHO WE ARE AND WHAT WE TRULY FEEL, WANT AND NEED RIGHT NOW.

My daughter had always been a model student. At fourteen years of age, she decided she wanted to be a doctor. During the school years prior to university, she worked hard to pave the way for accessing medical school, which only a few manage. We lived in England and, even with outstanding grades, students rarely receive more than a single offer of a university place and many candidates get none at all. She received four offers, which is incredible! We were very proud of her.

The first two years of her degree course went well; she achieved high grades and everything seemed fine. In the third year, two weeks after finishing the academic year and with just one essay left to submit, she quit. Perhaps she simply could no longer take the pressure she had been exposed to for the previous seven years.

There is no point in looking for someone to blame. As parents, we had never put pressure on her to choose Medicine - or so we believed. She alone had chosen that path. However, the good schools she had attended, the expectation nowadays for girls to be dynamic, a self-confident brother, parents who were successful in their professions, an assertive mother – that's where the pressure was coming from!

When my daughter phoned me in tears to tell me what she had decided, my answer was, "It's your life, so it's your decision. If what you're doing doesn't make you happy, I respect that decision. It was your dream to study medicine when you were very young but dreams can change. Life is full of opportunities and you have your whole life ahead of you. You will find your way." Even her brother tried to convince me to push her into continuing with the degree but that is not something I felt justified in doing and it would also not have been right to attempt to do so.

Each of us has to live with the consequences of our own actions, so we each must have the right, responsibility and freedom to choose our path.

In what remains of this journey, my purpose is to encourage you to look within - to discover new perspectives about yourself so that you can continue on your way with the inner peace that comes from knowing, understanding and accepting ourselves, and acting in coherence with the unique individual that we are. True self-awareness goes beyond our personality but, having already spoken of the importance of soft skills, the primary ability is the knowledge of our personality. This skill, although not often mentioned at work, is the foundation stone for developing all other skills.

> **IF OUR LEVEL OF SELF-AWARENESS IS LOW, WE ARE NOT ABLE TO FINE-TUNE OUR BEHAVIOUR WHEN INTERACTING WITH OTHERS, WHICH CREATES BARRIERS FOR BOTH PROFESSIONAL AND PERSONAL SUCCESS.**

Self-knowledge is not simply a skill you can take a course in, and then move on to something else. It is a constant process of self-observation, understanding and adaptation.

People are complex and have qualities that are not always obvious. The subconscious has a massive influence on our life, but the effects it can have are not easy to recognise. The subconscious affects everything that we are: identity, values, beliefs, feelings, thoughts, language and behaviour. Although we can never know everything about ourselves, if we pay attention we can recognise ourselves more objectively and we become less of a victim of our own nature.

Russian dolls, or matrioskas, could be a good simile to imagine how we can deepen our self-awareness. All parts of it make up the whole but, at the same time, each is individual in itself and at different depths. The further in they are, the more difficult it is to access.

FIRST LAYER: UNDERSTANDING HOW OTHERS PERCEIVE US

You'll find out how to put into practice what I have learned about giving and receiving feedback in chapter 7.

This aspect of self-awareness has been part of our work culture for years. We use feedback, or the perception of others, to adapt our behaviour and achieve better outcomes.

> THE MORE OPINIONS WE RECEIVE, THE MORE LIKELY IT IS THAT THE IMAGE WE HAVE OF OURSELVES WILL BE MORE ALIGNED WITH THE WAY IN WHICH OTHERS PERCEIVE US. FOR THIS TO HAPPEN WE NEED TO BE OPEN TO LISTENING, NO MATTER HOW DIFFICULT IT IS FOR US TO ACCEPT WHAT THEY TELL US.

The more we resist a particular criticism, the more likely it is that there is some truth we need to acknowledge. Furthermore, the things that drive us mad about others are often the things that direct us towards our own opportunities for improvement.

We all have some wonderful qualities and also some less positive ones which we often have a hard time recognising. Our willingness to accept these negative parts is essential if we are to foster self-knowledge; not to seek perfection or completely eliminate those characteristics that we do not like, but to learn to mitigate the negative impact that those aspects have on us and on the system of which we are a part.

SECOND LAYER: CONNECTING WITH OUR FEELINGS

During childhood we learn to hide emotions and throughout our lives we continue to repress feelings in order to survive and fit in. For that reason, although we do not always realise it, we can become disconnected from our feelings.

> ⚠️ WE TEND TO BE SO BUSY FULFILLING RESPONSIBILITIES THAT WE DON'T ALWAYS STOP TO OBSERVE HOW WE FEEL. THIS DISCONNECTION CAN HAVE SERIOUS CONSEQUENCES.

For some people, the inner emotional sphere goes unnoticed until there comes a time when this bottleneck of feelings explodes, leading to an extreme situation where a crisis, burnout, depression or a physical health problem appears.

Feelings have a mission to fulfill. If we are able to get up close and personal with them, they can help us detect what we need to change and, by paying attention to them, we will be able to manage our behaviour more effectively, improve relationships with others and make better decisions.

> ⚠️ WHEN WE ARE ABLE TO CONNECT WITH OUR EMOTIONS, THEY CAN RUN THEIR NATURAL COURSE INSTEAD OF BEING BLOCKED, THUS REDUCING STRESS AND INCREASING OUR HEALTH AND WELL-BEING.

📝 In chapter 13 you will find exercises that will help you connect with your feelings.

THIRD LAYER: KNOWING OUR STYLE OR PERSONALITY

Although each person is unique, there are personality archetypes that can provide clarity and understanding, as each of these archetypes has recognisable and common characteristics of style and behaviours.

There are different theories (such as the personality Enneagram or Clifton's strengths) and tools available. If you are interested in this topic, it is not difficult to find interesting and useful information. Getting acquainted with personality styles has several advantages.

> ⚠ PERSONALITY CANNOT BE CHANGED AND THERE IS NO PERFECT OR IDEAL PERSONALITY TYPE. ALL HAVE THEIR ADVANTAGES AND DISADVANTAGES.

We are all, to a greater or lesser extent, slaves to our personality style. We can recognise the behaviours inherent in it and identify the tendencies that we have, without realising it, when going about our lives.

If we are aware of our own tendencies, it is easier to adapt our behaviour, instead of letting ourselves be blindly carried away by our nature when it is not appropriate or beneficial to the situation. We can also focus on making the most of our strengths to get the best possible results.

Recognising the behavioural differences caused by each individual's personality can also help us become more tolerant and compassionate toward others. Sometimes we can be horrified because of what someone says or does, without understanding why they are acting in that way. Acknowledging that we all have different psychological programming helps us to accept other behaviours, even if we don't like them.

LAST LAYER: IDENTIFYING AND MEETING OUR NEEDS

In the deepest layer of self-awareness are our own needs, which includes living in coherence with ourselves.

> ⚠ OUR OWN NEEDS CAN BE HIDDEN UNDER THE WEIGHT OF EVERYTHING WE HAVE ACQUIRED OVER MANY YEARS: OUR PARENTS' DESIRES, THE NEEDS OF OUR PARTNERS AND CHILDREN, AND WHAT WE BELIEVE WE HAVE TO DO TO BE LOVED AND ACCEPTED.

Understanding this deeper layer requires reflection, introspection and sensitivity to identify what makes us unhappy. Some examples include when our environment doesn't adhere to the values that we subscribe to;

the work we do does not take advantage of our talents or requires skills that are not part of our natural strengths; or when we put on a mask that hides what we really feel and think.

Looking deep inside ourselves and glimpsing the needs that are truly born out of who we are, is the beginning of a beautiful love story; a story in which we take care of ourselves and at the same time we are able to take care of others, both at home and at work.

In my experience, many people turn to medication (or alcohol!) in an attempt to avoid the process called life, and in particular the changes needed to take care of our well-being.

I would like to tell you the story about the beginning of my journey of discovery into that last layer of my inner world. That journey that has undoubtedly led, for example, to my writing this guide which I am now sharing with you.

I clearly remember a night when I attended a concert with my husband. It was a beautiful summer night and a friend of mine was singing at a recital. I lived in the perfect place, had a good career, great children and a husband who loved me. And yet there I was, sitting on a red velvet chair, my husband lovingly holding my hand, trying to hold back my tears. I had a profound feeling that I can only describe as longing and emptiness: I was finally beginning to feel my inner self. The problem was that I had no idea what or who was the reason of my discomfort. I have a theory:

SOME EMOTIONS, WHICH WE SOMETIMES CALL DEPRESSION OR MIDLIFE CRISES, ARE OUR BODY'S WAY OF LETTING US KNOW THAT SOMETHING IS WRONG, THAT WE ARE NOT BEING HONEST WITH OURSELVES AND NEED TO MAKE SOME CHANGES.

You'll find strategies for managing your emotional states in Chapter 13.

I'm not suggesting that all cases of depression are for that reason but I believe the way to identify the cause of our emotional distress is to look within and, if necessary, make reforms. We need to find that coherence, even if the path does not always take us on a pleasurable, or apparently positive, journey.

Even when we are willing to find the strength to move forward by being brave and carrying out the changes, discovering the root of our discomfort is not always easy.

You might wonder why this is the case. The truth is that I do not know for sure, but after having acknowledged what was no longer making me happy and beginning a deep metamorphosis in my life, I will tell you what I believe from my experience.

There are issues that we don't allow to rise to the surface; repressed emotions that are uncomfortable; over-ambitious expectations of ourselves; the terrible 'I have to' that we whisper in our ear every step of the way.

> WHEN WE PAUSE AND OBSERVE, WE ARE AWARE OF WHAT IS HAPPENING TO US AND THAT WE HAVE ALWAYS KNOWN. IT WAS JUST MORE COMFORTABLE TO CLOSE OUR MIND AND STAY IN OUR COMFORT ZONE.

It's no wonder that so many people use antidepressants or other forms of avoidance to deal with that blockage.

You may be reading these words today and the voice within you is saying, "Yes, that happens to me," or not! Or you may have that feeling in your belly that tells you that you do know what you need to change ... or not!

It is possible that we have one of the four layers of the Russian doll more developed than the others but, by paying attention to all four layers, we can enhance our self-awareness and find happiness, both personally and professionally.

The dictionary defines self-awareness quite simply: knowledge and understanding of your own character.

In reality, self-knowledge goes much further and, in this context, I would take the definition a little further: the knowledge and understanding of our:

- Character
- Feelings
- Talents
- Desires
- Our body, and how it communicates with us
- Intuition

The brutal truth, I have discovered, from this journey of self-awareness (a few years after that night in the concert hall) is that when we finally realise what's wrong, things can get tougher before we start feeling better.

It's hard to know what you really want when there is a struggle between your desires and the inner voice that insists that it is not possible to fulfill them. We tell ourselves that it would be crazy, selfish, difficult, painful.

You will become intimate with your inner voice in chapter 14.

It is this struggle between the 'I have to' and our desires, that makes the feeling sharpen, transforming that longing and emptiness into suffering.

The good news is that once we are truly honest with ourselves and accept that this is the only way to move on, the suffering ends.

WHEN WE BEGIN TO MEET OUR NEEDS AND DESIRES, THE PAIN IS OVER AND WE ARE LEFT WITH A SENSE OF EMPOWERMENT AND PEACE.

I have changed a lot of things in my life in the time since that concert. Now, it's my time to act differently and pursue interests that provide me with a sense of fulfillment beyond what I had perceived as success at other stages of my life. It's not that I was previously wrong, but that my needs and priorities have changed.

In my case, I didn't become one of those people who have to resort to antidepressants. Even though, for some, that is the most appropriate route given their circumstances, I began a journey of self-discovery and change that has helped me become who I am today - the person I want to be, devoting time to matters that are important to me.

So, I'd like to leave you with something to think about, in case some of my words have made a mark on you today. When you feel emotionally unwell, before you try antidepressants, look within; you may find that all the answers are right there, staring you in the face.

I do not mean to trivialise the level of difficulty and effort that self-knowledge requires, but the reflection below will give you clues to identify what layer of the onion you are in and how to continue.

Score from 1 to 10 the following statements, with 1 being "Completely false" and 10 "Completely true":

When I think about who and how I am...

	Score
I actively seek feedback and opinions from others	
The feedback I get from others doesn't surprise me	
When I receive criticism, I understand their reasoning and accept it	
There are few behaviours in others that irritate me	
I am aware of how my behaviour affects others	
I know the most characteristic traits of my personality style	
I am aware of my strengths and the areas I need to enhance	
I am aware of my areas of development or weaknesses	
I easily identify my emotional states in different situations	
My lifestyle takes care of my personal needs	

- For each answer with a score higher than 7, write a concrete example that illustrates when you've demonstrated that.
- For each response below a 5, write a practical action you can take to foster this ability.
- Write down what you have become aware of by carrying out this exercise.

Seek feedback from people around you with this simple exercise, using this list of characteristics or behaviours:

Love	Calm	Disorder	Wrath
Sorry	Hope	Judgment	Abuse
Compassion	Empathy	Fear	Maltreatment
Acceptance	Confidence	Complaint	Insecurity
Peace	Creativity	Pride	Frustration
Gratitude	Spontaneity	Fault	Sadness
Generosity	Indifference	Anger	Discouragement
Humility	Patience	Attachment	Tension
Joy	Assertiveness	Grudge	Lie
Freedom	Tolerance	Jealousy	Agitation
Decision	Goodness	Resignation	Intolerance
Solidarity	Enthusiasm	Vanity	Vengeance
Vitality	Motivation	Apathy	Rigidity
Proactivity	Eloquence	Doubt	Laziness
Capacity	Simplicity	Control	Shyness
Commitment	Leadership	Rivalry	Avarice
Union	Harmony	Punishment	Arrogance
Service	Honesty	Comparison	Selfishness
Responsibility	Order	Envy	Worry
Availability	Charity	Distrust	Possessiveness
Warmth	Abundance	Exclusion	Ingratitude
Sympathy	Amiability	Irresponsibility	Lack
Flexibility	Brotherhood	Indifference	Impotence
Charisma	Respect	Submission	Chaos
Safety	Diplomacy	Justification	Dependence
Faith	Work	Coldness	Humiliation
Discernment	Sincerity	Impulsiveness	Reservation

- Go through the list and use a marker to highlight those words with which you most identify.
- Send the list (unmarked) to several people and ask them, from their perspective, to choose the three words that most characterise you in a positive way and three that you could work on.
- Compare the words you chose with the ones which they have chosen.
- Write down what you have become aware of by carrying out this exercise.
- Choose three words from the list that you would like to enhance in your behaviour and one that you would like to integrate from now on. Write them down, display them somewhere visible and put them into practice in your daily life.

Chapter 10

YOUR INTERPRETATION OF THE WORLD

If you've read all the pages that precede this one, with all the stories I have told you and the reflections I have shared, I imagine that you have inadvertently created a picture of me in your head. Who am I? Is it a question or a riddle? Let's play a little with this idea to introduce this chapter.

As we saw in the first part of this book, the outside world is obviously important, especially if you are in that vital stage in your life when you want to forge your career and grow professionally and financially.

We strive to learn how to manage our environment so that we can offer what is required from us by that outer world.

> WE ACT PROFESSIONALLY AND TRY NOT TO LET PERSONAL PROBLEMS AFFECT OUR WORK WHICH CAN SOMETIMES LEAD TO OUR BEING SO BUSY LOOKING OUTWARDS THAT WE DON'T PAY ENOUGH INWARDS ATTENTION.

The inner world is an intrinsic and inseparable part of what we project outwards. My proposal for you, in this second part of the book, is to explore those aspects of our interiors - subtleties that are able to make the difference between success and failure, enjoyment and stress, evolution and stagnation. In a nutshell - between feeling good or bad.

Let's go back to the question of who I am. That is a very good question. In fact, it is a question we often ask ourselves. This question has a variety of answers throughout life and is more than a question. I would say it is a puzzle with endless possible solutions.

One of the definitions of a riddle is: "A question that is seemingly difficult to understand, asked as a game and which has a surprising answer."

So let's play. Before you continue reading, think or write three words that describe your impression of me so far. The first ones that come to mind. Don't let your mind take over. Let your instincts guide you. Go ahead and make a note.

15, 10, 5... Your time is up!

Congratulations! You just thought of a few things about yourself. The way you see me, and the silent assumptions you have made, say more about you than they do about me. They give you clues about the prejudices that you unknowingly have.

I have made a hobby of identifying my own prejudices - and other things - about myself. My journey into self-awareness has been revealing and every day I try to continue discovering new answers about myself. This observation process was the first step towards rethinking some of my beliefs and changing my perspectives. Thanks to this, I began to live differently, with less unhappiness and more self-appreciation.

So, let's see if it is possible to learn something about *yourself* by revealing some aspects about *myself*.

Since I turned 21 years of age, I have lived in 7 cities and 12 houses, had 12 jobs and travelled to 23 countries: yes, you could say that I have 'itchy feet'. Regardless of how much time we spend on each chapter of our lives, the important thing is to be committed and motivated about what we do, no matter how long each phase of the journey lasts.

I am an accountant by profession and during my career I have been climbing the ladder through many different roles which multinational companies offer within finance. In England it is common to make jokes about accountants, calling them 'dull' or 'boring', but I'll let you be the judge of that.

> ⚠️ IT IS IMPORTANT TO BE YOURSELF AND NOT TO BLINDLY FOLLOW ANY 'RULES OF THE GAME' ARBITRARILY IMPOSED UPON US, OR THE STEREOTYPES THAT SOCIETY HAS OF THE CHARACTERISTICS THAT DEFINE US FROM THE OUTSIDE, SUCH AS OUR JOB, NATIONALITY, GENDER OR PHYSICAL APPEARANCE.

Going back to the question of who I am; I am many things. We all are – including you.

> ⚠️ WHO WE THINK WE ARE IS THE RESULT OF A LIFETIME OF LISTENING TO OTHERS, AND TO OURSELVES, TELLING US WHO OR WHAT WE ARE.

> ⚠️ THOSE LABELS MAY BE APPROPRIATE AT TIMES, BUT WE DON'T NEED TO TURN THEM INTO A CAGE.

I have learned that although our personality affects us considerably, it is also possible to make our own choices. We can try new activities and may well surprise ourselves. If we give ourselves permission to let go of preconceptions about who we are, we begin to discover new identities, areas of interest, talents and desires.

For example, I recently discovered that I love writing poetry. I was stunned, especially considering that I have never liked poetry and thought that creativity was not one of my strengths. However, here I am, writing poetry from time to time and really enjoying it.

So now that you have some more information about me and you, how accurate do you think the words you chose at the beginning were?

I close this reflection by encouraging you not to take the preconceptions you have about yourself and others too seriously and to see what interesting surprises come out of the magician's hat. Doing so you can let go of some labels that do not serve you, daring to see yourself from renewed perspectives.

Let's take a closer look at how, without realising it, we have a biased view of our experiences. I'll use another riddle. What does a WhatsApp have in common with maths?

"When we read a WhatsApp, our mind can add, subtract, multiply or divide."

Think about how many WhatsApps you have sent that have been misunderstood.

I would like to share with you a quote from Carl Jung, the renowned psychologist, who said: "Everything is mediated through the mind, translated, filtered, allegorised, twisted, even falsified by it." Clearly Jung was very perceptive and knew a lot about how we think and operate.

It is impossible for the brain to process everything around us. In an attempt to manage the excess of information, we could say that the intellect becomes lazy and begins to find shortcuts to interpret what surrounds us. To create all these shortcuts, it uses strategies influenced by connections that are buried deep within our subconscious.

Any Whatsapps you may have thought of are a good way to illustrate that 'what we interpret about the world is not what is really there' or, as we say in neuro-linguistic programming, 'The map is not the territory'.

Of course, there are plenty of reasons why we do this and proper examination of this requires more time than this chapter can devote to it. For this reason, I would like to focus on some filters that have a massive impact on our daily lives.

Thoughts, also called internal dialogue, are like the soundtrack of our lives and create the atmosphere of the experiences we have.

Let's use an exaggerated example: how do you think you would feel watching a Disney movie with horror-film music playing in the background? Becoming aware of our internal dialogue allows us to shape it favourably and be more neutral in our interpretations of the world.

Culture or beliefs also create distortions in words, behaviours and symbols. The symbolic representation of good and evil has different meanings depending on where we come from. A swastika is a good example of this, as it has been banned in many contexts in Europe, given its association with World War II, whilst in Asia it is a symbol of divinity and spirituality.

> ⚠ **RECOGNISING THAT AN ABSOLUTE TRUTH DOES NOT EXIST HELPS US HAVE FEWER PREJUDICES.**

Our emotional state, born out of our thoughts and beliefs, plays a huge role in interpreting what we experience.

> ⚠ **NOTICING HOW WE FEEL AND TAKING IT INTO ACCOUNT TO CONTEXTUALISE BEFORE WE REACT IS LIBERATING.**

For example, when we are in a good mood, the sun seems to shine brighter and when we are depressed, all we see are dark clouds on the horizon.

So where am I trying to get with all this?

Self-awareness is a long journey of discovery. Learning to identify what filters or shortcuts we use to interpret the world, allows us to get to know ourselves better, be more balanced in our interpretations and become the beautiful people we are within.

When we acknowledge that our opinion is only one of many possible options, we can be open-minded about the position others take and be less reactive in our day-to-day interactions. It can also be a feeling of relief that we don't always need to be right. Ask yourself:

- What do I choose, being happy or being right?

So the next time you have a negative reaction to a WhatsApp, email, or other communication, pause for five seconds and ask yourself if the filters you have used are cloudier than usual. And, when in doubt, just ask!

Identifying the biases we have is not easy. However, paying attention to our language is a fantastic way to get to know ourselves. In this way, we discover how we distort the world and the filters we apply to life through the words, thoughts and styles we use when talking to others.

WE USE LANGUAGE IN THREE WAYS WHEN OUR POSITION IS NOT NEUTRAL AND THERE IS A BIAS. SPOTTING THOSE WAYS CAN ALERT US TO THE FACT THAT WE ARE NOT BEING OBJECTIVE.

The first way we use language for this purpose is when we generalise. For example, when someone says, "Pretty girls are shallow," this is a generalisation and not an absolute truth if we think about all the girls we've met who are pretty.

The second way is omission. For example, when we say, "I was hurt by his words." Not every word the other person said hurt you. This statement may be true, but only partially. Which word or words in particular hurt you?

The third case is when we distort. For example, when we say that one thing leads inevitably to another. I remember when a friend told me, "Every time I leave the car parked, I forget where I left it." I looked into her eyes and asked, "Are you really telling me that you never remember where you parked the car?", and we laughed.

By paraphrasing what we say in an exaggerated way, we are able to laugh at ourselves and become aware of how ridiculous the 'claims' we sometimes make can be.

We say things without really considering our choice of words and without becoming aware of the hidden meanings that our language can reveal. I used to start many of my sentences with an apology, until a colleague pointed it out to me and from that moment on, I began to notice it more and more.

I even apologised before expressing my opinions and for taking up someone's time. As soon as I noticed this, I began to wonder what was behind those apologies and began to realise that maybe I needed to value myself more.

Why did I feel the need to apologise for asking others for time when I tended to be generous with mine towards them? In the end, although it is not language that reveals questions about ourselves, asking ourselves what is hidden behind that language does.

For example, one day I went for a walk and bumped into a friend. We greeted each other briefly and within seconds she said, "Oh, I'm on my way to meet a friend to go for a walk together." She was making excuses for being alone.

The excuses we make also betray what happens in the privacy of our subconscious. Why do we feel the need to explain or justify certain circumstances to others? We can get deep insight by paying attention to the pretexts we give.

Another example: when I told someone that I had recently separated, I always automatically added, "But it has been an amicable separation." The interesting thing about my offering that explanation was that it was really no business of theirs at all, but that I still felt the need to make it clear to them that it had, in fact, been amicable.

Was it because of my sense of guilt or my fear of being judged for ending twenty-five years of marriage? Or perhaps because of my own self-judgment?

These questions do not have a single answer but thinking about it can contribute to increasing self-awareness. Ask yourself:

- What is behind my language?
- What apologies and excuses do I make?
- What do I strive to make clear to others?

When we look behind those points that we try to make clear to others, we find insecurities and fears; how little we value ourselves in certain respects, as well as what we do value and what we believe in. Ask yourself:

- How do I usually react when someone gives me something?
- Do I find it difficult to accept a compliment or act of kindness and just say, "Thank you."?

Asking questions is another powerful way to find out. That is why I hope you have been doing the exercises on each topic throughout this book. We often know more than we think and all we need is to take the time to sit alone and reflect. I do it using a journal which I write some mornings. If you have never had a journal, you really should try it - it is very rewarding. Creating the habit can be quite difficult but doing it daily, even if all you write is a couple of pages, is a good way to make it part of your daily routine. Find the time of day that works best for you: in my case it is as soon as I wake up.

Powerful questions can turn on the lights and give us insights into aspects that we have not yet noticed, whether they are instigated by someone else –

for example, during a coaching or mentoring process – or by simply asking ourselves, even if we are not entirely neutral.

The answers to powerful questions have the ability to point us towards the changes we need in our life, the aspects we really enjoy, or the direction we need to take. So I encourage you to question your assumptions with the exercises proposed in this manual - or as your intuition dictates.

In summary, bias is inevitable when our personality tries to make sense of the world around us.

> ⚠️ **PAYING ATTENTION TO THE PHRASES WE USE IS AN EFFECTIVE WAY TO IDENTIFY WHAT BIASES WE HAVE AND OTHER FEELINGS HIDDEN IN OUR SUBCONSCIOUS.**

These biases influence our thoughts, what we say to ourselves and others, and reveal some of the deeply-rooted beliefs we have; convictions that, although born out of a good reason, no longer have anything to contribute to our life. By seeing them clearly, it is possible to begin to make conscious decisions about maintaining such beliefs or letting them go if they no longer serve us.

To do this exercise you will need several days:

- Listen carefully to the conversations you have and identify possible generalisations, omissions and distortions.
- Take note of phrases or expressions that catch your attention in what you say or hear.
- Pay particular attention to what you say about yourself to others.
- Observe yourself and identify situations in which you justify yourself or become defensive.
- When you have a few sentences written, for each of them:
  ‣ Try to identify the hidden bias or belief they denote.
  ‣ Re-write the belief or bias in a positive way, or question its value.

Example 1 — You told someone: "I am terrible at public speaking" — Denotes the belief: "I am not able to speak well in public" — Neutralised belief: "I lack confidence when speaking in public, so I could learn."

Example 2 — You begin sentences with: "Excuse me or I'm sorry, but" — Denotes the belief: "My contribution is annoying or inadequate" — Neutralised belief: "My contribution is valuable and I will stop asking for forgiveness when it is not appropriate".

Chapter 11

MAKE YOUR CHOICE AT ALL TIMES

For this chapter, I recommend that you find a gap in your day when you have enough time, are rested, and feel in the mood for some self-enquiry. Find a comfortable place and prepare your favourite hot drink. If you feel some reluctance, that's normal. Set that aside and get on with it. Are you ready? Well, let's go for it!

I believe that balance is the key to much of what we do in life - that optimal point between opposite poles where magic starts to happen - that balanced spot between work and rest, Yin and Yang, strength and vulnerability ...

Even though I have that belief, one thing I have learned is that the optimal place is not always the middle ground but, in fact, being able to change our position within the available spectrum to find that point of equilibrium. That is, making our choices each and every time regarding what is the place between one extreme and the other, as required by the circumstances.

We all have personal characteristics that we demonstrate every day. Some of them we label as good while others we classify as bad. We have already covered that a unilateral and absolute vision of any situation is not the most accurate one.

> ⚠ ALL OF OUR CHARACTERISTICS, REGARDLESS OF THE LABEL WE HAVE ASSIGNED THEM SO FAR, HAVE THE POTENTIAL TO BOTH IMPROVE AND HINDER HOW WE PERFORM AT WORK, AS WELL AS IN OUR PERSONAL LIVES.

When appropriate, it is important to find the break-even point. However, at other times it is more advantageous to take a standpoint but remain mindful of both possible extremes. So the intention of this chapter is to prompt you to reflect on some aspects of your personality so that, if there are areas in which you are stuck in a particular position, you can consciously choose, in each separate scenario, which behaviour works for you. And remember, it's not about changing ourselves but about not being slaves to our personality and nature.

AT WHOM DO YOU POINT THE FINGER?

One of the characteristics that divides personality styles is whether we tend to attribute responsibility for what happens to external factors or to ourselves.

People who point their finger outwards often blame what happens on others. "Dinner was burned because I received a phone call," "I have not delivered the report because department X did not provide the information I asked for," "I did not get the position because the person who interviewed me did not ask me the right questions," ...

People who point their finger at themselves tend to blame themselves for everything that happens. "That client did not accept the proposal because I made a terrible presentation," "Dinner was burned because I am a disaster," "I have not been promoted because I screwed up in the interview," ...

Reality is undoubtedly somewhere between the two extremes. Whatever our natural tendency, recognising the way we usually react helps us get closer to a healthy point which allows us to evaluate situations as they are. It is easy to recognise this tendency; we only need to use our ears.

I remember candidates I have interviewed who did not get the position they were seeking because, among other reasons, they clearly demonstrated a tendency to point the finger outwards during the interview, which does not inspire confidence in others.

On the other side of the spectrum, putting the full weight of responsibility on our own shoulders can weigh on us emotionally, as well as giving the impression to others that we think the world revolves around us.

So, if you are still not sure which side you tend to take, listen to yourself in the coming days carefully and you will surely find out.

Think of a recent failure:

- Describe it in a few words.
- Write about the reasons with which you justified what happened to yourself or to others.
- Look again at what happened and describe new subtleties regarding responsibility that you had not previously recognised.
- Write down what you have become aware of by carrying out this exercise.

PATIENCE

Do you rush or delay things?

I strive to be patient, as it is not one of my strengths. I have always been a proactive person; in my world everything happens fast, which is good because this gives me the impetus to advance in the workplace and in my personal life. For example, the penultimate time I moved house, only two weeks had passed from when I saw the house for the first time until the moment I signed the deed of purchase and moved in. I don't hang about!

Having said this, I recognise —and I am aware — that patience is also a positive and even a proactive trait to have in life. Patience gives us time to reflect, produce polished work and act after carefully thinking things through. It also gives others time to keep up with us on projects that we lead, to get them where we want them to be.

Although I my natural tendency is to be proactive, quick and impatient, I now value patience. I try to practice my patience to be able to enjoy the benefits that it brings me, striving not to be carried away by my nature.

At the other end of the spectrum, I have found myself in situations where initiatives have come to a grinding halt. Indeed, some people are so patient that the necessary actions are never carried out at all.

So, like everything in life, it's about knowing when it is appropriate to act swiftly and when to have patience. When we don't act, we lose momentum, and a sense of urgency can give us the drive necessary for us to carry out our projects. If we take too long to take action, we waste time and opportunities, and even when we achieve what we set out to do, it may no longer serve our best interests. The difficulty, of course, lies in establishing when it is the right time to be one or the other.

When we put off making changes, making difficult decisions, or getting down to business, it can be a symptom of avoidance or resignation rather than patience. It is useful to recognise where our actions come from.

Ask yourself:

- What do I feel: impulse, resignation, fear, adrenaline, patience, laziness?

I am still looking for that discernment. I do this by taking the time to take safe steps toward a specific purpose while moving quickly enough to be effective.

[!] **THE FIRST STEP TOWARDS ENABLING OUR DISCERNMENT IS TO RECOGNISE THE PHYSICAL SENSATIONS THAT MANIFEST IN OUR BODIES WHEN WE HAVE THESE AUTOMATIC REACTIONS.**

Do you recognise the feeling I'm referring to? It happens with everyday experiences.

One day I was chatting with my sister on the phone and she happily told me that she had found a house that she would like to buy. While talking to her, it occurred to me how I could help her to complete the purchase successfully. The idea caused an all-too-familiar feeling: a tingling in the stomach that always makes me want to rush into things, filling me with excitement and enthusiasm. Noticing the sensation, I said to myself: "Susana, don't tell her anything yet, check with your partner and sleep on it. If it still seems like a good idea tomorrow, you can call her and tell her."

Achieving this simple ability to put the brakes on an impulse required years of minor and major moments of regret for having rushed into something. The eureka moment came when I was finally able to identify the bodily sensation that accompanied those moments.

[!] **IT IS EASIER TO IDENTIFY THESE BODILY SENSATIONS THAN THE AUTOMATIC RESPONSES THAT DIRECT OUR BEHAVIOURS, SO THEY CAN BE OUR SIGNAL TO PAUSE AND THINK.**

The exercise at the end of this section will guide you towards identifying your particular sensations, which you can then use as an alarm system when looking for that point of equilibrium we talked about earlier.

A simple strategy when you recognise that sense of urgency is to ask yourself: 'Can this step wait a few minutes, hours or days?' If the answer is yes, pause before acting. That interval will give you the opportunity to reorganise your thoughts and correct aspects that will enhance your initial impulse and if nothing new appears in that period of caution, it will allow you to move forward with confidence, having created that safety net.

So ask yourself: how patient am I? Am I patient in the right way? You may be surprised by the answer.

Think about recent changes or projects:

- Describe a step you think you rushed into or regretted after you took it.
- Write about things that were not considered during your decision and that would have contributed to a better outcome.
- Close your eyes and remember how you felt at that moment just before you took that rash step. Take your time and pay attention to the memory of that sense of urgency in your body.
- In the coming days, pay attention to your behaviour and identify when that feeling you remembered appears again. That is the time to pause and go over the situation before continuing.
- Describe a step that you think you are procrastinating about without good cause.
- Write about the aspects or barriers that hold you back from taking the necessary steps.
- Close your eyes and remember how you felt at that moment of doubt that prevented you from acting. Take your time and pay attention to the memory of that feeling of avoidance in your body.
- Write about the possible consequences of continuing to freeze that next step.
- Take note of the conclusions that come to mind by carrying out this exercise.

RELUCTANCE

We have talked about the importance of not procrastinating too much. Life would be simpler and less fun if we could always apply the same rules. Let's also explore reluctance a little, so that we don't only label it as an enemy, because it also has the potential to be our friend.

Reluctance could be defined as resistance to do something before you do it, because you don't want to do it or because you're not sure it's the right thing to do. I love dictionaries - some definitions are fantastic!

> 🔔 **RELUCTANCE HAS TWO COMPONENTS: ONE HAS TO DO WITH ATTITUDE AND THE OTHER WITH INTUITION. THEREFORE, WHEN WE FEEL RELUCTANCE, IT IS POSSIBLE TO TRANSFORM IT INTO A TOOL TO IDENTIFY WHICH PATH TO FOLLOW.**

Understanding what's behind our resistance can spring us into action, thus transforming reluctance into a catalyst.

We do countless tasks every day: we get up early, take the dog out, attend that meeting at nine o'clock, do the household chores ... some of them with resistance.

Reluctance is like a shadow; something that obscures what we do, robbing us of energy and enjoyment. It takes away the opportunity to enjoy the day and do our tasks well and with enthusiasm. Use it as a guide to let go of procrastination and take the appropriate steps.

The first step is to identify which elements or tasks you carry out reluctantly and classify them into two groups: those that have advantages at the end and those that leave a bitter taste in our mouths. For example, even if you don't feel like exercising, you feel great afterwards; or when you leave the office late for the thousandth time you feel resentment towards your boss.

With this perspective it is possible to review your attitude towards the things that bring you value. If you want to continue doing them, that resistance does not bring you anything, so stop messing around and get down to work with a smile on your face when they are due. There is a difference between saying and doing something, I know. There are strategies, such as self-reward, after you carry out other activities that give you pleasure. For example, when I feel lazy about writing these pages, I make a commitment to myself to spend two uninterrupted hours before having some coffee and a piece of my favourite chocolate.

After identifying those activities that do add value, you can focus on those which do not contribute as much. Here you can find opportunities for improving your situation and the impetus to start thinking about what to do about them. You have four options:

- Do nothing, which is not my favourite option.
- Accept them and stop wasting energy resisting.
- Abandon them, if possible.
- Change them by taking steps that benefit you. Small steps sometimes lead to big breakthroughs - having a conversation, setting boundaries, asking for support or finding a middle point.

Make a list in the exercise below and go for it!

When you take stock in this way, you will enjoy the feeling of taking action, even if you'd rather avoid it, knowing that it is good for you and that you have done everything in your power to improve your situation. This way you will face the activities ahead of you with less reluctance, feeling more positive and taking more control of your life.

How many things do you do reluctantly every day?

- Start by making a list of everything you do.
- Once you have the complete list, identify the ones you do with resistance.
- Classify tasks into two groups: those that add value and those that don't.
- Assign each task that does not add value one of the four suggested options: do nothing, accept, abandon or change.
- Write down your conclusions about this exercise and make a list of next steps or actions that you think are appropriate.

I CAN!

One of the activities I postponed for too long, thanks to my tendency to procrastinate and putting my job too high on my list of priorities, is practising yoga.

I'll tell you how I finally managed to break that trend in chapter 15.

In one of my yoga classes, I was trying to do a new pose, one of those that really puts your body to the test. I felt pain in the joint we were working on but, being the way I am, I maintained the position for as long as the teacher wanted, despite the pain it was causing me. My breathing and the beads of sweat on my forehead gave me away and another student looked at me and said, "Susana, are you okay?"

"Yes, of course, I just find it hard," I replied, rather defensively, "but I can do it!"

And suddenly I realised that I'm pretty stoic. How many times have you said, "I can," despite being under a lot of stress, pain or difficulty?

In fact, during the exercise I was not okay. I needed to either stop doing it or have the teacher show me how to improve my posture. Reflecting on this situation, I realised that the cause of this attitude is one of my beliefs: 'Being stoic is a good thing.' Our personal beliefs can be found lurking behind many of our more extreme behaviours.

If we can identify behaviours that don't feel right and stop to think about what they mean and why we pursue them, we have the opportunity to reset our attitude towards them. In this way, we approach the healthy balance that we desire and improve our experiences.

Let us continue with this example of stoicism. One definition of stoicism is: "The quality, condition and characteristic of being stoic, that is, one who is strong, serene and courageous in the face of misery or misfortune, in being tolerant, resigned and in accordance with circumstances." When I looked up the definition via Google, reading it made me laugh and realise that, like many things in life, it is a coin with two sides.

Of course, it is good to maintain serenity, face the difficulties of life and accept some challenging situations. But, at the same time, everything has its limit, especially when we move too far in one direction or another. It is important to know where our healthy ceiling lies, after which that 'I can' no longer helps you get what you want but harms you personally.

> ⚠ IF WE ARE NOT ABLE TO IDENTIFY THAT TIPPING POINT, WE CAN PUSH OURSELVES SO HARD THAT WE CAUSE OURSELVES HARM. THE REPERCUSSIONS ARE EVIDENT IN OUR HEALTH, OUR EMOTIONAL STATE, OUR PERSONAL RELATIONSHIPS - IN SHORT, IN OUR LIFE.

For this reason, taking time to reflect on the negative aspects of the usually positive characteristics of which we're proud, gives us a cold shower of reality which, although uncomfortable, is the path to the appropriate point where we enjoy the best of ourselves without being harmed.

Returning to the example of stoicism and having considered these subtleties, I conclude with my adapted definition: "Balanced stoicism is to be strong, to have serenity and to maintain one's spirit in the face of misery or misfortune, with tolerance, resignation and acceptance of the circumstances, but has to stop at the point where it starts to harm us."

> Another interesting aspect of self-exploration is our tendency toward rationality or emotionality. In chapter 13 we will further explore your emotional world.

We could explore many characteristics and investigate where our natural response lies within the range between the opposite standpoints but it is not necessary. The most important lesson about this work of exploration that we're undertaking is acknowledging that there are no perfect or ideal positions for every moment of our lives. When we can recognise our usual mindset but also value the virtues of the opposite position, we can make our own choice instead of reacting automatically, becoming truly free.

For this reason, I would like to conclude this topic by encouraging you to redefine some of your concepts and create your own definitions according to how you want to live your life because, when we are truly aware, we can set our own rules.

Think of yourself:

- Make a list, quickly and without thinking, of words that describe you as a person.
- Break that list down into attributes that you consider positive and negative.
- For the positives, write about the negative consequences they might generate or entail.
- For the negatives, write about the positive consequences they could have.
- Write down what you have become aware of by carrying out this exercise.

Chapter 12

DON'T TURN A BLIND EYE TO YOUR DARK SIDE

Our tendencies and behaviours cover a wide range of possibilities, for instance, being generous and being stingy depending on the circumstances. In this chapter we will explore many variables to find that things are not always what they seem.

It is natural for us to turn a blind eye to our own actions when we have feelings or behaviours that are undesirable on the set of values we subscribe to.

> ⚠ IF WE IGNORE THE ASPECTS WE DISLIKE, WE LOSE PERSPECTIVE ON HOW WE ACT. IN ADDITION, SOME OF THESE ELEMENTS THAT WE REFUSE TO ACKNOWLEDGE ARE CHARACTERISTICS THAT, WELL CHANNELLED, CAN ADD INSTEAD OF SUBTRACTING.

Looking in the mirror to face those unattractive sides directly, without makeup, is part of our personal growth, so let's look at ourselves.

> **⚠** WE GO THROUGH FIVE STAGES WHEN WE LOOK STRAIGHT AT OUR DARK SIDE: BLINDNESS, DENIAL, SHAME OR GUILT, COMPASSION, AND ACCEPTANCE.

ARE YOU SURE YOU ARE THE WAY YOU THINK?

We start out being totally blind to our behaviours. This state of total ignorance may be very comfortable for us but it will certainly generate conflicts with others. In this state, we receive reproaches from others which we deny, truly believing that we are right, when reality may be quite different. There are thousands of examples and the signs can be seen even in our day-to-day family lives, such as when one partner says to the other, "You always leave the toilet lid up," and the other thinks, "It's not true because I usually put it down." This is a mundane example of those occasions when we act without awareness, because the person doesn't "always" leave it up but often does so without being aware of it.

Going beyond tangible examples, our dark and unconscious side manifests itself in ways that we do not always see: jealousy, self-centeredness, aggressiveness, narcissism, lack of empathy, etc.

For example, for years I have prided myself on not being a jealous person. However, a few years ago at a training event, I discovered to my astonishment that I am definitely capable of being *really* jealous. I'll expand on this later in the chapter - we have more subtleties than we think!

One way to open our eyes and start to see those aspects that we do not recognise is to ask ourselves, "What do I boast about?" This is something of a cliché, I know. In fact, in Spain there is a well-known saying; "Tell me what you boast about and I will tell you what you lack."

Another way to discover our blind spots is to observe what behaviours irritate us in others. It is possible that we actually do some of the annoying things ourselves without realising it or, on the contrary, we fail to take the right action because we don't give ourselves permission.

In a job I had, the behaviour of one of my colleagues irritated me. I felt that he was narcissistic and selfish because all he thought about was how to get what he wanted for himself and his team. He was tireless in his self-promotion. He really annoyed many of us, as some colleagues called him 'The meritologist.' I started to wonder why I was so irritated by him when I normally get along with everyone. I came to realise that his pushiness was not an attitude which came to me naturally, nor had I allowed myself to acquire it. For example, if I had been more openly forthcoming about my achievements, I could have taken more opportunities to convey my value proposition openly without feeling embarrassed.

When we stop being totally blind to our weaknesses, the natural tendency is to deny what we have already perceived or what we had a feeling about but had not acknowledged openly.

In the section about language giving us away, we talked about the excuses we make without realising it. In the same way, those words we use to introduce ourselves to the world are an opportunity to find out what we don't accept. For example, a phrase I've used often in the past was "what you see is what you get."

The Enneagrams provide an interesting methodology to look in the mirror. I discovered them by chance and they helped me to tie up some of the loose ends in my personal discovery process. I concluded that the Enneatype I mostly identified with was number 3. This category is described as encompassing those who wear the mask of 'a winner'. People in this group strive to project the image that we want to project to the outside world, hiding our true needs from everyone - even from ourselves. Ironic, don't you think?

The Enneagram of personality is a methodology in the field of humanistic psychology for the study of personality. Although it has ancient roots it evolved through different psychologists and developed more widely by Claudio Naranjo. This model classifies personality styles into nine Enneatypes, with three possible subtypes in each of them.

THEY SAY THE TRUTH HURTS

Alas! When we realise that a behaviour that we thought was only present in others is also present in us, we can be overwhelmed by feelings of guilt. At that point, we hit rock bottom. How embarrassing! How shameful! How horrific!

When considering the different personality styles, it is important to add that within our natural behaviour, there is a spectrum. That is, we can act in a certain way with more or less emphasis. When we are at ease and balanced, we speak of being in a 'healthy' state and we demonstrate our tendencies without exaggeration. This is the sweet spot, when we are being authentic without being led astray by any of our personality tendencies towards exaggerated reactions and behaviour. However, lack of balance or neurotic behaviour manifest when we are under pressure or in difficult emotional situations.

I remember when I came to the conclusion that, indeed, my personality style, according to the Enneatypes, was a '3', I felt like a fake. I had prided myself all my life on being honest and transparent and it turns out that my style, when I'm not well, is to hide what I feel or think. Ouch!

Wallowing in remorse is of no use. It is best to take whatever steps we deem necessary to repair the damage if possible. For example, we can be more careful with lowering the toilet lid or recalibrating our behaviour so we don't let the same dog bite us twice. However, the best thing we can do when we can see ourselves without a mask is to look forward and stop beating ourselves up.

Don't underestimate how hard it is to recognise our dark sides. Recently, in a workshop I teach, I had a conversation with a participant. We were talking about this issue of recognising these hidden parts. She said she was not a stingy person; that she was generous. She was adamant that she was generous and, after a discussion on this subject, I asked her:

"So, are you generous with yourself?"

"Oh, no, the truth is that with me, I am stingy," she replied, thoughtfully.

"Well, there you have your stinginess, even if you don't always show it openly to others."

COMPASSION IS A PATH TO FORGIVENESS

When our personality takes over, resulting in regret, if we take the time to stop to think about it, we can identify that in reality such behaviour is caused by a weakness. Whatever our 'sin' is, when we start pulling the thread, we find fears that feed that behaviour - fear of rejection, humiliation, abandonment, betrayal, injustice. (If you find this topic interesting, there are psychology books that talk about the wounds of childhood).

⌐!⌐ WHEN WE OBSERVE OUR OWN VULNERABILITY AND THE FEAR THAT FEEDS THOSE BEHAVIOURS THAT WE DO NOT LIKE, IT IS POSSIBLE TO CONNECT WITH THE CHILD WHO IS DEEP INSIDE US AND CONTINUES TO INFLUENCE THE REACTIONS WE HAVE.

⌐!⌐ WHEN WE ACKNOWLEDGE THAT WOUNDED CHILD, IT'S HARD NOT TO FEEL COMPASSION FOR OURSELVES AND OTHERS.

Let's go back to the example of my envy. I remember the first time I recognised those feelings in myself in a social situation and paid attention to how I felt physically. It was during a residential training course that lasted for two weeks. We were a diverse group of people with no apparent reason to be competitive with each other. During a dinner, while a colleague was talking and the others were paying attention to her, I realised that this undeniably uncomfortable feeling was envy. What nonsense! How could I feel jealousy!?

Reflecting, I realised that this vaguely familiar feeling had visited me when interacting with certain people in different parts of my life. In a job not so long ago I had felt it towards a colleague with whom I had had some clashes; in another, towards my boss to whom I felt inferior. When I was a teenager, I felt it with those friends who were more attractive or fashionable than me. And the list can go on ... Realising that I had indeed been jealous, I connected that envy with difficult situations in my personal and professional past. Thus, I concluded that these feelings, which were unconscious and often irrational, had been an obstacle and generated difficulties. Digging into the cause of this jealousy I came across 'Susanita', the girl, who felt insecure and not pretty enough. The vulnerable feelings we've all had as children continue to accompany us for years. How can we not feel compassion for the wounded children we all carry inside?

> ⚠ THIS COMPASSION CAN BE FOLLOWED BY FORGIVENESS, WHICH FREES US TO TAKE A LIGHTER PATH INSTEAD OF MAKING US FALL INTO THE SAME TRAPS. AS SOON AS WE BECOME AWARE, THESE PATTERNS DISAPPEAR FROM OUR LIVES.

WHAT WE HIDE IS NOT NEGATIVE

> ⚠ THE THINGS WE HIDE ARE SOMETIMES THE TALENTS THAT WE STOP NURTURING AT SOME POINT IN OUR PAST.

It is not uncommon for us as children to conclude that we are not good at some skill if a project was met with criticism or lack of interest. Consequently, it is also interesting to review the limiting beliefs we all have, such as, "I am not a creative person," or, "I am terrible at writing, painting, dancing …"

See what you can pull out of your magician's hat. When you explore your qualities, I encourage you to also investigate positive aspects that are hidden. A few years ago, my writing this book was unimaginable. However, by exploring new ways of understanding myself and leaving behind old beliefs, I have managed to surprise myself with my creative skills. If you'd like to delve into your creative capacity, which you may have hidden, I can highly recommend a book called *The Artist's Way*, by Julia Cameron. It is an excellent tool to help you explore this area. Through her writings I discovered, not only that I am able to write and enjoy poetry, but many aspects of myself that had been hidden.

MIRROR, MIRROR ON THE WALL …

I hope you found some of your hidden faces in this chapter.
There are, of course, behaviours that often arouse negative reactions: manipulation, control, overprotection, victimhood, indifference, etc. The list is endless.

Let's take manipulation as an example, something that for years drove me potty when I saw it in others. Do you tend to manipulate others? Are you sure?

From time to time, we complain that others manipulate us or try to force us in some way to do what we don't want. There are several forms of physical or emotional manipulation. Manipulation can play a part in many interactions and without knowing how, we are persuaded to do what the manipulator wants. Those being manipulated become frustrated, although they are not always aware that they *are* being manipulated.

Not all styles of manipulation are evident. We can all be manipulative without being aware of it and can hide that tendency behind a seemingly harmless smile, as I have realised by looking in the mirror.

In this chapter my intention is to promote your self-exploration, making you look in the mirror from an alternative perspective. Hence, I encourage you to question the different manifestations of the behaviours that bother you in others to see if, with humility and compassion, you see your true reflection in the mirror.

The good news is that just as it is difficult for us to recognise in ourselves the characteristics that we do not like but easy to see them in others, exactly the same thing happens with the qualities we admire. When we see other people's merits, the reality is that they also hide within us.

So, do you know your hidden behaviours and talents?

> ⚠️ **THE HIDDEN ASPECTS OF OUR PERSONALITY DESERVE TO BE DISCOVERED AND HELP US TO LIVE A FULFILLING LIFE.**

Let's welcome those aspects within us. When we are able to admit to having them and recognise those aspects that we do not like, or do not allow ourselves to admire, we are free to stop being victims of our own personality.

Think about the conversations you have with others:

- What descriptions do you use regularly about yourself? With what taglines do you justify yourself when talking? Make a list, for example: honest, generous, transparent, fair, etc. Make sure that you include positive and negative attributes in the list.
- With the list of positive attributes, reflect honestly and ask yourself: do I practice these behaviours always and towards myself?
- Write down some specific examples which illustrate how you have demonstrated these qualities.
- With the list of negative attributes, reflect and ask yourself: when was the last time I put this belief to the test?
- Think of someone who arouses antipathy and make a list of the things you dislike about this person. Reflect honestly and ask yourself: if there

were no repercussions or sense of guilt, would you like to behave like this person in some of those aspects?

- Think of someone who arouses admiration and make a list of the qualities you see. Reflect objectively and ask yourself: aren't these qualities also within me?
- Describe your conclusions or new perspectives after the previous exercises.

WELL-BEING

What a ride!

Now that we're embarking on the last leg of this journey, we will talk about the last element that I consider essential for everything else to be sustainable: well-being.

We'll get up close and personal with your emotions and we'll delve deep into the facets of your ego to empower you so that you can be consistent with your needs and take care of your health.

Chapter 13

CONNECT WITH YOUR EMOTIONS

I imagine that although you have professional and economic aspirations, like almost everyone, you also want to be happy.

> [!] NO MATTER HOW GOOD WE ARE AT MANAGING THE OTHER AREAS, IF WE WANT TO REACH OUR POTENTIAL WITHOUT RISKING OUR HEALTH AND WELL-BEING IN THE PROCESS, WE NEED TO INCLUDE THIS DIMENSION IN OUR DEVELOPMENT PLAN.

Happiness has a multitude of meanings. I could write a chapter about what it means to be happy but the result would be my own personal conclusions. What we are aiming for here is for you to find out what happiness means to you, enabling you to take that as your compass to guide you along every step you take in your life and in the decisions you make each day.

Let's start by thinking about what wellness means. One definition I found was that it is the things that are necessary for us to live well. I think that's an excellent starting point. One of the fundamental assertions in this guide is that although it is fantastic to have professional

ambitions and pursue them, it is not worth achieving them if, in the attempt, we fail to feel good and enjoy the journey.

For me, beyond having my basic needs met, well-being means having a good emotional and physical state. To achieve those two elements we need to properly manage the rollercoaster of feelings that life presents us with and take care of our body.

EMOTIONAL STATES

Emotions have a massive influence on our life experience. Sensing and expressing feelings is easy for some people but difficult for others. Regardless of which group you fall into, the sensations are there whether we acknowledge them or not and learning to recognise and digest them can help us to feel better instead of getting blocked.

It has been theorised that there are only five basic emotions - happiness, sadness, fear, disgust and anger; all others being simply different shades of those. We can also summarise them into just two: love and fear. Are you able to identify them when you feel them? Whilst this may seem like an absurd question, it is not. It is possible to hide our emotional states, not only in front of others but also to ourselves. For example, I have a hard time expressing anger and when I block it, it generates accumulated discomfort and frustration. When I had an existential crisis, which happens to many of us at some stage, I realised that for a long time I had been blocking my emotions. I had been so busy working, looking outwards and focused on my to-do list, that I hadn't stopped to notice how I felt.

If you haven't seen the Disney movie *Inside Out*, I recommend it. It illustrates with simplicity the different types of emotion and shows that they all have a function to fulfil.

> 🗨️ WHEN WE RECOGNISE AND ACCEPT EMOTIONS AS STATES AND NOT WHO WE ARE, THEY GUIDE US ALONG THE WAY INSTEAD OF PUSHING US TOWARDS DESTINATIONS WE DON'T WANT.

Sensations are not only felt but also transmitted, so the organisations to which we belong are loaded with whatever impressions prevail within the group. If you think about companies where you have worked, and teams or people with whom you relate, you can surely identify which emotion prevails.

When we recognise the emotional influence that some environments and people have on us, we can act to modify those interactions or, if necessary, abandon them. There are people I've worked with who exhausted me physically and emotionally because of the way I thought and acted around them. I remember a colleague of mine who, although I liked him as a person, he was like a cancer in the organisation. Every conversation he had spread bad feelings around him with complaints, criticism, negative comments or teasing. My perception was that if the toxic atmosphere he was projecting was exhausting for me, it must have been at least equally exhausting for him.

> 💬 **WE ARE LIKE RADIOS EMITTING WAVES OF VIBRATION, CAPABLE OF RAISING THE FREQUENCY AND NOURISHING THE SYSTEM OR LOWERING IT, TO EVERYONE'S DETRIMENT.**

An interesting book that talks about emotion in all its manifestations is *Letting Go*, by David Hawkins. This book is unusual because it addresses the issue of feelings and consciousness from a clinical and also a spiritual perspective.

Keep a journal for the next 7 days to identify your emotional states. Score from 1 to 10 these statements, with 1 being "Strongly disagree" and 10 "Completely agree":

		Score
Happiness	I feel happy	
	Yesterday I had a nice day	
	Today I'm going to have a good day	
	Average	

Sadness	I feel sad	
	There are aspects of my life that make me depressed	
	I'm having problems	
	Average	
Fear	I feel afraid	
	I'm blocked	
	There are threats in my life	
	Average	
Disgust	I feel reluctant	
	There are elements in my life that I dislike	
	I reject something around me	
	Average	
Anger	I'm fed up	
	I have negative feelings towards others	
	There are circumstances in my life that frustrate me	
	Average	

Upon completion of the 7 days:

- Describe how you have felt, or have expressed, the five emotions physically in you.
- How have positive feelings manifested in your behaviours?
- How has negativity manifested in your behaviours?
- What emotion has predominated during the week? What factors do you think contributed to this?
- Which feeling has been least present? What factors do you think contributed to this?
- Write down what you've acknowledged by doing this exercise.

SELF-ESTEEM

Once we acknowledge our emotions, we can begin to take care of our mental health - and self-esteem has a great role to play.
Let's start this section with a confession: I get bored by doing the same thing over and over again, which can cause me to lose interest in important topics.

We feel great when we believe in ourselves and are confident that we're going about things in the right way. We could say that this feeling of worth is like the water in a swimming pool: it is not good if the Ph is too high or too low. It's necessary to add the appropriate chemical components to regulate it. External factors and our insecurities are responsible for lowering self-esteem so, although this is not always the case, some effort is required to raise it.

It is nice to recognise our positive qualities. It is also healthy to balance that vision by integrating, with kindness towards ourselves, aspects that are not so positive.

> ⚠️ HEALTHY SELF-ESTEEM INCLUDES BEING AWARE OF OUR STRENGTHS BUT ALSO OF OUR WEAKNESSES OR QUALITIES THAT CAN LET US DOWN: MOMENTS OF LAZINESS, FEAR WHEN FACED WITH CHALLENGES, DARK FEELINGS, OR INEXPERIENCE WHICH LEADS TO MISTAKES.

There is a very nice part of The Serenity Prayer, by Reinhold Niebuhr, which says, "God grant me serenity to accept things which cannot be changed; give me courage to change things which must be changed; and the wisdom to distinguish one from the other."

Feeling good about oneself is not an infinite source of satisfaction for possessing only wonderful qualities but the strength of knowing what capabilities we have to support ourselves on life's journey, what aspects we are striving to improve and what aspects we accept about ourselves with humility and compassion.

Let's go back to the confession I started with. Having tried to modulate that aspect of my personality, I have not yet quite succeeded so I have learned to mitigate the impact of my tendency to get bored by carefully choosing the projects I work on and the members of my team, ensuring they have traits and skills that I am not so strong at.

Self-confidence is a must. When we feel self-assured, we transmit that feeling to those around us, making them more likely to support us and give us new opportunities.

We are not born with confidence. We construct it like a tower, stone by stone, using our life experiences as the building blocks. We have an infinite number of resources and every day we have the opportunity to use them to show ourselves and others that we are capable.

Even when we think that we have healthy self-esteem, this may not always be the case. I remember one occasion, quite late in my professional career, when one of my mentors told me, "Susana, you have everything, but you lack confidence". Self-esteem is something tangible that others detect and, as long as we do not cross the line into arrogance, it is important to nurture it every day. Arrogance, at the far end of the spectrum, is always undesirable so you should be careful not to sound conceited or boastful, especially when you are talking to others. Even if you feel (or feel the pressure to show) that you are superior to the people you're working with, try to retain and express some humility.

Starting to recognise the capabilities we have is a good way to foster authentic confidence based on our strengths. In this way, we will be true to ourselves and honest with others. I hope that throughout this book you have used a diary of reflections. If you haven't already, this is the time to start.

- Buy yourself a notebook that you can use as a diary.
- Boost your confidence by using it to write down your positive thoughts and what makes you proud.

> 🗨️ **IT IS NOT ABOUT PRETENDING TO BE SOMEONE WE ARE NOT, OR BEING ARROGANT, BUT ABOUT BEING HONEST AND PUTTING ASIDE THE EMBARRASSMENT OF ACKNOWLEDGING THE POSITIVE BECAUSE WE HAVE OVERRIDDEN OUR INNER CRITIC.**

> In the next chapter I will tell you how to make peace with your inner critic.

We all suffer crises of confidence and if we allow ourselves to be carried away by those doubts, we can lose momentum.

What does self-esteem mean to you? Feeling confident at all times is not a realistic ambition. Being willing to take a step forward, even if we are not 100% sure, is a great achievement. Let's value the positives we already possess instead of pursuing perfection.

Think of a recent situation where you've felt out of your comfort zone:

- Describe the circumstances in a few words.
- What resources or personal skills did you put into practice to face what was happening?
- What additional resources do you have that you didn't put into practice?
- What beliefs do you have that make you think that this situation tested your limits?
- Write statements about those beliefs.
- Review those claims and question their veracity.
- Write down what you've become aware of by doing this exercise.

No matter how much emotional intelligence and self-esteem we have, feelings will continue to have an influence on us. These sensations are like the weather: there are many kinds and they are always changing. As we saw before, an important part of wellness is recognising that we and our emotions are not the same thing. If we return to the example of

the weather, we are like the earth - stable and impassive - and emotions are the events that come and go - storms, heat waves, hurricanes, monsoons and so on.

How do you feel today? As we saw in the first part of this chapter, every day we experience many different states. The positive ones are, of course, pleasurable while negative ones can be hard to bear. Being aware of them at every moment is invaluable. Thus, instead of simply letting ourselves be carried away by the wind direction of our storms, it is possible to learn to manage them.

[!] AN ESPECIALLY USEFUL STATE TO RECOGNISE IS OUR CRASH STATE. THIS STATE IS CHARACTERIZED BECAUSE WE ARE CLOSED, REACTIVE, ANALYTICAL, SEPARATE AND HOSTILE.

[!] THIS STATE PREVENTS US FROM SEEING THE SITUATION IN A BALANCED WAY, PROPERLY MANAGING THE ENVIRONMENT AND FEELING GOOD.

The CRASH state was defined by NLP professionals, and its opposite is the COACH state (Centred, Open, Aware, Connected, Holding). You can dig deeper with the works of Stephen Gilligan and Robert Dilts.

CRASH states manifest differently in each person. Our style depends on our personality and the moment we are at in our lives. My CRASH state causes me to hide away, feeling sad and isolated from others. Other people may explode, expressing anger and frustration.

Knowing how to identify our own states of discomfort is important. When we are in a CRASH state we are not objective and the thoughts we have are reactive. It is likely that a feeling of isolation is not due to a real rejection by others and that our anger is not entirely someone else's fault. Being attentive and realising that we have gone into CRASH allows us to manage our response by taking a deep breath, not saying rash and regrettable words or postponing a decision.

So ask yourself: when I CRASH, how do I usually express myself? How do I feel?

Once you are clear about your pattern you can identify it, take a step back and get out of it more quickly in your day-to-day life.

Let's do it. Think about the last situation where you've experienced a CRASH state. Don't think too much – just the first one that comes to mind.

- Describe in a few words the circumstances that led to that state.
- Describe how you felt in those moments. Think about your feelings and how they physically manifested in you.
- What reaction did you have or what did you do because of that emotional state?
- Review your description of the circumstances and correct it, if appropriate, to express it as objectively as possible.
- What could you have done differently if you hadn't been so immersed in the emotional bubble?
- How will you recognise that CRASH state when you experience it again?
- Write down any other thoughts that you find relevant in these circumstances.

If you frequently find yourself in these situations, it would be enlightening to take note of when they occur. In my case, for years I have gone into CRASH when I was at work and at moments when I felt particularly insecure. I finally realised that they coincided with the dates of my period and, even though they kept happening, I was able to take a step back to observe those sensations instead of allowing them to completely overwhelm me.

The triggers are as varied as there are people and situations, so - have you taken a step back?

It is possible to encounter the same failure or emotional state over and over again in any project, challenge, pursuit, relationship or conversation.

In the moment just before these failures lies the key to how to resolve them, although it is not always easy for us to see it. That small detail may be what we have to do differently to achieve our goal.

Think about a CRASH situation in the last year:

- Describe what was happening before you entered that CRASH state.
- What can you do differently to prevent or mitigate that trigger?
- Write down what you've acknowledged by doing this exercise.

Chapter 14

GET TO KNOW THE CHARACTERS OF YOUR EGO

Do you know that feeling of emptiness in the stomach when you realise that you have made a mistake and all you want is to disappear?

That is how I felt one day, when I started reading the comments left on the company's intranet in response to the micro-Valentine's Day gift we had presented to hundreds of employees spread throughout the Iberian Peninsula.

That initiative, which should have been one of the star moments of the year, had become a nightmare. In my position as Director of Corporate Services, I was responsible for human resources and there was a lot to do. We wanted to change the culture of the company from one that in the past had been guilty of treating workers as replaceable pieces on a chessboard, to an organisation that promoted personal well-being so that people felt valued. A noble purpose and undoubtedly admirable, but which had many obstacles to overcome.

We came up with the idea of sending a heart-shaped lollipop to all the employees on Valentine's Day. The intention was to celebrate this day together in a fun way without having to make a financial investment that we could not afford. Two of my colleagues worked for hours to carefully prepare all the packages which were despatched from our head office and sent to all of our stores. We were very excited.

When the photos and smiles began to be published on the company's intranet you could feel the atmosphere of celebration. We felt pleased that this small gesture had brightened the day of many colleagues.

Big mistake! In our eagerness to take care of the staff, we (myself included) had not considered that in the chain there were people beyond the corporate staff who were part of the franchise network of stores.

By mid-morning, complaints and unpleasant comments began to appear. You can imagine how I felt when I began to realise that this initiative that we carried out in good faith and with so much enthusiasm, had backfired and came back to bite us. Some of the franchisees were horrified by our lack of sensitivity by not including their employees in the initiative. Comments like, "to save spending a few measly cents," were made.

For me, the worst thing about this experience was not the complaints, but the campaign of self-reproach and remorse that I waged against myself. I was upset for weeks. I couldn't get the incident out of my head or the thousands of 'should's.

From an objective point of view, I knew that what was done, was done - and that I gained nothing from reproaching myself. With my team, my attitude was at all times one of support and focus on learning. However, with myself, in my mind's eye, I was a real tyrant.

The inner voices, always present in our lives, are travel companions with whom we share smiles and tears.

⚠ THESE WHISPERS CREATED BY THE EGO SERVE SEVERAL PURPOSES: TO GIVE REALITY TO ITS EXISTENCE, TO DEFEND OURSELVES FROM THE THREATS WE PERCEIVE, TO ENCOURAGE US, TO PUNISH US, TO JUSTIFY OUR ACTIONS, TO CONSOLIDATE BELIEFS AND ULTIMATELY TO SEPARATE US FROM THE WORLD OF WHICH WE ARE AN INDIVISIBLE PART.

These voices are not objective, they are reactive and change throughout our life's evolution, so they do not represent who we really are. Whatever we are, regardless of the spiritual beliefs we subscribe to, is constant and immovable.

When we start from the premise that our true essence and the ego are different components, we can begin to experience, at times, the different versions of our ego as observers rather than protagonists.

Our behaviours and interpretation of what happens to us are influenced by those characters who, like the strings on a puppet, control what we feel, say or do. Starting to feel those threads is a big step towards freedom. From this position of the observer, it is easier to maintain the connection with our personal essence. Self-talk becomes an ally rather than your own worst enemy, as if you were able to wake up in the dream and direct the chain of events.

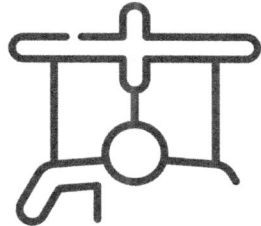

⚠ IDENTIFYING OUR CHARACTERS AND RECONCILING WITH THEM IS AN ESSENTIAL PART OF OUR PERSONAL DISCOVERY.

Life is like a theatre play with a group of actors playing their roles through our internal dialogue and where each one has different connotations. We play countless characters: hero, judge, boycotter, executioner, caretaker, winner, etc., etc., etc.

All these masks that we wear, both 'the good' and 'the bad', are nothing but manifestations of the personality that characterises us, even if we only like to identify with the positive ones. I believe that there are three modalities that deserve to be considered: torture, judge and boycott.

TORTURE

This behaviour is that scratched vinyl that goes around endlessly and although it is not easy, it is possible to stop it. I propose two different strategies to counteract this tendency, although it is not necessary to put both of them into practice. The first is pausing your thoughts and the second is shifting your focus to something positive.

> ⚠ **THE ABILITY TO PAUSE THINKING IS ONE OF THE HEALTHIEST SKILLS WE CAN PRACTICE.**

This has several names: prayer, mindfulness, meditation, state of alert, 'knitting' or climbing. The name and the form do not matter; the important thing is what all these techniques have in common. They calm the mind and help us get closer to our most essential part.

The state of a calmed mind is a source of well-being which we can turn to in times of difficulty. To achieve this, it is not necessary to go on a retreat in Tibet; you just need a little discipline and will power. Five minutes a day of practice is enough to create the habit of calming the mind.

A simple way to calm the mind is to focus on your breath and the five senses, as fully as possible, feeling all the perceptions at once. This is a technique taught by Krishnamurti, called 'unitary perception'.

To create the habit, it is preferable to look for a time of day that works for you; first thing in the morning, after breakfast or before your daily shower - it doesn't matter. Look for that gap that is repeated in your natural routine to reserve those five minutes that can bring you so much well-being.

Do not pursue perfection. There will be times when you try and it will be a disaster because your mind will be full. Don't make a fuss; just keep trying and on another day it will be easier. The goal is not to meditate, but to stop and try.

Once you have created that habit, you can have meditation moments anywhere when you need it.

Record the instructions below in a loud enough voice, clearly and calmly so you can practice afterwards listening to the recording:

- With your eyes open or closed, start focusing on your breathing. Feel how the inhalation fills your lungs reaching your belly and how the exhalation relaxes your body.
- Keep feeling your breath, every inhalation and every exhalation deeply. At the same time feel your skin, the sensation of your clothes touching your skin, the air on your face, your body in contact with the chair or the floor.
- Feel the sounds around you without judging them, whether soft or loud, or just the silence.
- Whilst you concentrate on your breathing, your touch and your hearing, add the perceptions you have with your eyes. If you have your eyes open, relax them and simply let the images penetrate your retina. Without any judgment; just feeling them. If your eyes are closed, feel the flashes or darkness you perceive behind your eyelids.
- Continue to feel, deeply, all those perceptions that your senses give you. Now also feel the taste in your mouth, of something you have recently eaten or just your saliva.
- Feel your breath, your skin, the sounds, the images, the taste.
- Identify the smells around you, the people around you, the food nearby, the air coming in through the window; feel the smells.
- Continue to feel everything at once, without judging whether they are good or bad, pleasant or unpleasant, feel the experience, like a child who feels without knowing.
END OF RECORDING.

- Whenever you want, listen to the recording to focus on the feeling of all your senses and continue in silence for a few minutes. You will notice that by feeling, your mind calms down and your thoughts will be less persistent.

Changing the focus of our thoughts is the second strategy. When you notice those harmful thoughts that distress you, let them pass or change them by focusing on something positive that inspires you.

You can use a memory that produces a feeling of well-being, visualising that moment or sensation at critical moments. This will lower intensity of your mental torture. This strategy is no different from what we do with young children when they hurt themselves or are misbehaving and we try to divert their attention by saying, "Ooh! Look at the ... ".

Think of a place where you've felt happy, quiet and safe. You can read these instructions slowly while you do this exercise or record them to do the exercise later with your eyes closed.

- Visualise that special place, taking note of the shapes, colours and brightness it had.
- Remember the sounds around you: people, animals, the wind ... soft or loud sounds ...
- Take a deep breath and remember the smells you smelled. Plants, people, the sea ... Subtle, intense, fresh ...
- Integrate the flavours you experienced at the time - food, flowers ... sweet, refreshing, penetrating flavours ...
- Feel the place, the objects you touched and felt on your skin or with your hands - clothes, a breeze, the sofa ... texture, temperature ...
- Now choose a colour that represents all those sensations that you lived in this special moment and, seeing that colour, make a small movement that connects you with this memory. A gentle touch on the cheek, rubbing your fingers - you choose.
- Breathe deeply and feel the well-being in that moment with all of its components, colours, flavours, sensations and sounds while everything has a hint of the colour you have chosen and, at the same time, make the small movement that you chose.
END OF RECORDING

This simple exercise, called 'anchoring', has etched a memory in your body associated with that colour and gesture. When you are in situations of discomfort, if you think about the colour and make the gesture, you will observe how the intensity of the negative emotion in your experience decreases.

It is possible to reinforce the intensity of your positive anchor by repeating the exercise or simply briefly remembering your colour while making the gesture regularly.

You only need a few seconds to reinforce positive messages in your brain, so the more you do it, the easier it will be for you to get out of negative thought patterns.

Thoughts can be trained, just as we do with our body. The more negative or positive thoughts we have, the easier it is for us to continue using those mental connections. It's up to you to reinforce one pattern or another.

THE BOYCOTT

This character is the one who tells you, "You can't," "Don't try," "Others do better." We usually call it the 'imposter syndrome'.

The imposter torments us about different things, depending on our situation, but often focuses on certain areas. "I am a mess," "I am fat," "I have no willpower," "They're going to notice that ...", "I'll get fired," "I've done that terribly." "I've screwed up!" The list of examples could be endless.

If there are discouraging messages that you frequently tell yourself, write down empowering affirmations which contradict those messages and tell them to yourself when you go into a self-torment loop.

> [!] AFFIRMATIONS ARE A SIMPLE WAY TO TAKE A STEP BACK AND DEMONSTRATE TO BOYCOTTERS THAT THEY ARE NOT RIGHT.

Think of a situation where you usually torture yourself with your thoughts:

- Write down the sentences you say to yourself.
- Write statements that contradict these reproaches and more statements that go further. Give yourself compliments, tell yourself what you are worth, how much you are loved, all that you deserve.
- Choose a few of these statements and write them down in your reflection journal for 21 days, starting each day with, "Today I choose ..."
- If new ideas of empowering affirmations occur to you during this process, add them to your list.

THE JUDGE

This guy is the hardest to catch! When interacting with the outside world we analyse everything around us. Part of this mapping includes forming opinions or judgements about absolutely everything we encounter. It is as if we spend our lives labelling things as good or bad; right or wrong; desirable or undesirable. It is such a normal thing that we don't even realise what we're doing.

This behaviour is natural and helps us navigate the world we live in, making decisions and guiding our actions as if we had a compass. In this regard opinions are useful but they may also have undesirable effects.

Our opinions or judgements never represent the absolute truth because it does not exist. They depend on our past, our personality style and the information available to us, which is always incomplete.

Some people are particularly prone to negatively judging others, turning their attention to their shortcomings rather than their virtues. One of my bosses continuously picked up on the faults of his team members and I was sure that he was also picking up on mine, even if he did not tell me. One person was not proactive enough, another not strategic, another had no potential and so on. The reality is that all the people around him had strengths and weaknesses. The fact that he gave free rein to his internal judge was unfair to others and also damaged his personal experience, making him feel unhappy with his team and leaving him frustrated.

Furthermore, those who are prone to being overly critical of others tend to judge themselves just as harshly, if not more so.

> ⚠️ LIVING UNDER THE TYRANNY OF A DEMANDING INTERNAL JUDGE CAUSES US PAIN AND MANIFESTS ITSELF IN INSECURITIES, RIGIDITY AND STRESS.

So the next time you observe something or someone and make a judgment, ask yourself:

- What do I gain by making this judgment?
- Would everyone agree with me?
- How does this judgment apply to myself?

AND NOW WHAT?

Once you have identified the mask of your personality in its many guises, give it a name and recognise that it is not really you, and that it is not always right. I gave mine a rather unattractive name, and, whenever I notice its appearance, I say to myself, "Here we go, ***'s turned up!" No matter what name you give it, by doing so you can become the observer and see the character.

The next step is reconciliation. Even if it doesn't support you, that inner voice has an inherent positive intention; probably to protect you. It was formed in your childhood to help you to survive and adapt to the environment you were in. It is not about blocking this part of us but about understanding that it is something natural with which to make peace and learn to overcome.

[!] WHEN WE BECOME RECONCILED WITH OUR CHARACTERS, THEY APPEAR MORE SELDOMLY AND WE FEEL MORE LIBERATED.

Pay attention to that voice in your daily routine to bring to your attention how often you go into a loop of negative thinking and, when you do, stop yourself in your tracks. Adding a touch of humour to any learning process can be very helpful and make things much more memorable, so perhaps it might help if you could visualise a favourite cartoon character frantically waving a 'Stop!' sign at you.

The first step is to recognise what is happening and the second is to make the decision that you no longer need to react to the little voices that echo from our past. To free ourselves from that tyranny is wonderful for us and for everyone around us. Try it!

Chapter 15

ACT COHERENTLY

Well-being is not something we can force; we find it little by little when our actions are consistent with our feelings and thoughts. Our challenge is that, as we have seen in previous chapters, thoughts and emotions are not always right, so finding true coherence is not so easy. However, one way to get closer to it is to identify our true needs and take care of them as best we can.

> **WHEN WE PUT OUR NEEDS BEHIND THE OBLIGATIONS, BELIEFS AND PEOPLE IN OUR LIVES, WE ARE NOT COHERENT WITH OURSELVES.**

We can take care of our needs in a thousand ways. Although in this chapter I examine several that have been particularly useful for me, they are as varied as each one of us.

Think about the tasks you had lined up for this morning and ask yourself:

- How many are for the benefit of my personal well-being?
- What things am I doing where the mask I show to the outside world is different from the thoughts and feelings I have inside?

I do not mean to suggest that we should always put ourselves above all else, but if we do not learn to take care of our own needs in the right measure, we will not only be causing ourselves harm but we will also be betraying ourselves because of a lack of coherence and, as we will see ...

> ⓘ THE IMPORTANT THING IS NOT WHAT WE DO OR HOW WE DO IT BUT WHERE THE DECISION TO DO IT COMES FROM.

I propose four important considerations for this topic:

- Choose when to give or negotiate.
- Identify when you need help.
- If it doesn't serve you, let it go.
- And what if you can't let go?

CHOOSE WHEN TO GIVE AND WHEN TO NEGOTIATE

Consciously choosing between giving and negotiating is a good step to take care of our needs.

Are you a person who gives a lot? There are personality types that are prone to being caring, generous and to putting a lot of effort into their interactions or life projects. This attitude has advantages because it can lead to having good times and it is possible to do a great job and achieve our goals. So far so good, but, beware: if we negotiate when we think we are giving, there is a large price to pay by everyone involved.

> ⚠ GIVING CAN BE ACCOMPANIED BY AN UNCONSCIOUS LABEL OF VALUE, BECAUSE IN REALITY WHAT WE SEEK WITH THAT BEHAVIOUR IS TO RECEIVE; FOR EXAMPLE, BEING ACCEPTED, LOVED, AND, ALTHOUGH WE MAY NOT REALISE IT, THAT ACT OF GIVING IS ACCOMPANIED BY AN EMOTIONAL DEBT.

Deep down, what we want is for that person, situation, or job to give us back the effort we have put in. Sadly, life doesn't work like that. What we give does not always come back to us as what we would like to receive. We create expectations that are neither appropriate nor realistic, it being impossible for others to settle all those mental bills that we have been issuing.

Since we were children, we have been taught what is acceptable for every type of relationship and throughout our lives we've been drawing up our own list of requirements. For example, in Spain there is a joke about not choosing a boyfriend who wears white socks with shoes. Although it seems a bit comical, there are expectations that are cultural or that belong to a different time in our lives which no longer serve us - aspirations that for each relationship or project are as irrelevant as they are useless.

It is important to know what our boundaries are, because there are people and circumstances that are unable to contribute what we consider important.

> ⚠ WE CAN TRANSFORM OUR EXPERIENCE INTO SOMETHING POSITIVE SIMPLY BY RE-EVALUATING OUR EXPECTATIONS AND MAKING SURE THAT WE AREN'T REACHING FOR THE MOON.

When we negotiate instead of giving, without being aware of it, we feed a deep sense of disappointment that can cause us sadness which can also lead to losing interest with what we are involved in. This is a shame because, despite your having 'given a lot', it could result in the failure of that relationship or initiative.

It is not a matter of your rational mind wanting to give less, but about giving freely, learning to ask and also to receive. It's also about spotting when is the optimal time to question our motivation because we are constantly giving in order to feel good, essential, superior or needed.

When we give with the expectation of receiving, we end up being disappointed. At first, we're completely oblivious because, by giving, we are happy and feel great but there comes a time when we begin to notice that we are not receiving and that the scales are not balanced. This is when we start to feel bad.

In an ideal world it would be good to know how to stop before reaching this point because sometimes the damage is already done by the time we start to notice. A good strategy to help us to take care of ourselves is to pause before giving and question ourselves as to whether we are giving or negotiating. Ask yourself:

- What am I hoping to achieve through this?

If it's simply because you want to, or because you're going with the flow, go ahead. But if you look at your motivation, you may realise that what you're really doing is investing or trading; not giving.

To give freely means to give without agenda or expectations in the workplace, relationship or project. If you choose to negotiate, and that exchange suits you, recognise the transaction for what it is and surrender instead of resisting. When we negotiate, we pursue a win-win for both parties and if it doesn't suit you, it is a good time to be candid and put a limit on what you are willing to offer.

IDENTIFY WHEN YOU NEED HELP

Identifying when we need support is another big step towards starting to take care of our needs. However, we don't always realise that we need help, especially when it relates to responsibilities which we have agreed to take on personally.

I have a great friend and colleague who, for many years, has given everything she could at work to the point of reaching physical and emotional exhaustion, working long hours during the week and often during weekends as well, always putting her work-related duties before her own personal well-being. She is a committed person who has always provided good results to her line managers, and is one of the most responsible and committed people I have ever had the opportunity to work with. The temptation, of course, when you reach the point when you can't take it anymore, is to blame the company, the role, the line manager, colleagues or subordinates. But when this situation seems to stalk us from one position to another, we have to ask ourselves:

- What am I doing that does not favour my circumstances?
- What do I achieve by working so hard?
- What am I gaining by maintaining this situation?

Reluctance to ask for help, or to say, "I can't," has the potential to have serious effects on our performance and also on our health. If you work in a busy office you will have experienced or observed situations in which meeting the demands and expectations of the job is practically impossible, especially if you do not have someone to assist you. If we are not able to assess the situation and realise that we need external support, we can swim upstream until the quality of what we do suffers or we even get sick with overexertion and stress.

To ensure that we get the support which is necessary, I put this methodology to you in four steps:

- Get off the hamster wheel.
- Identify your needs.
- Set healthy boundaries.
- Go for it.

GET OFF THE HAMSTER WHEEL

On many occasions I have told my team, "Oh, we need to get off the hamster wheel." By that, I meant that when we are so caught up in the spiral of our

situation we are not able to see our position clearly. Thus, we are unable to fully see the horizon and what may be evident to others, whether they are challenges or opportunities. Likewise, the internal boycotter assumes the usual role that we know about: "You are weak," "You have to try harder," "You will be fired," etc.

TO BE COHERENT WITH OUR NEEDS, IT IS NECESSARY TO TAKE A STEP BACK, GET OUT OF THAT HAMSTER WHEEL AND OBSERVE OUR CIRCUMSTANCES MORE OBJECTIVELY SO THAT WE CAN STOP SWIMMING UPSTREAM.

As laudable as your intentions may be, if you continue in that wheel you can only exhaust yourself without reaching any destination. Returning to the example of my colleague, her dedication led to her moving to different companies several times but every time, within a matter of months, her feeling of being overwhelmed quickly became unsustainable again, because she was unable to get off her wheel.

For this reason, I encourage you to imagine yourself on a hamster wheel when you feel overwhelmed so that you remember to take that step back and evaluate your circumstances.

IDENTIFY YOUR NEEDS

To find the right kind of help, the first step is to identify our needs:

- What exactly is my problem?
- What barriers stand in my way?
- What tools do I need?
- Who has the capacity to meet my needs?

Whilst solving the problem entirely may not be possible, we can identify viable steps to mitigate the impact. Breaking it down into its components is beneficial. For example, in the case of my friend, she might have wondered:

- Are the tasks I carry out effective?
- Am I doing tasks that I could share or delegate?
- Is it all equally important?
- Do I work at the same pace as other people around me?
- Am I overexerting myself?
- And if I do, am I giving or negotiating?

Identifying your needs will lead to possible solutions, which will make things easier for you when the time comes to find help.

SET HEALTHY BOUNDARIES

This is undoubtedly the most difficult of the four steps because it is hard for us to set limits and maintain them. There was a time in my career when I was in this situation myself. Every week I promised myself that I would leave the office at a reasonable time in the afternoon. I even put a reminder in my diary to remind myself when to go home. Day after day, week after week, the reminder popped up at seven o'clock in the evening only for me to ignore and continue to go about my tasks.

The type of limit to be established will depend on the circumstances but, in any case, although it is difficult to take the steps to mark our boundaries, it is important to try to be firm in our efforts.

On one occasion, I had a person working in my department who was quite similar to the friend I mentioned earlier. We were working under pressure and in adverse circumstances. I saw how stressed she was every week and her exhaustion became more and more evident. In one meeting I explained that, given the circumstances, it was not possible to do everything and I emphasised that the unfinished work was either my responsibility or that of the whole team; not only hers. I asked her kindly to accept that there would always be incomplete tasks. She had the habit of taking her laptop home and she continued to work every night after dinner, despite my insistence that she needed to put her well-being ahead of the to-do list. Hence, I suggested that she should help herself by leaving her laptop at the office and thus create a healthy boundary.

Scheduling spaces to deal with unforeseen events is also beneficial. In a conversation with one of the people I mentor, he said:

"I never get home on time because I don't start doing my own work until six o'clock in the evening. During the day I have a lot of meetings and I also have to support my team when they are faced with unforeseen events."

I asked:

"So, do you get asked for help about unforeseen issues every day?"

He confirmed that he did. There was silence for a few moments and finally he continued. "Well, maybe they're not so unforeseen. The topic changes, but the demand for my time is always present."

"Well, then, why don't you leave some space in your schedule to enable you to support them, even if you don't know what the issues will be about? Worst case scenario, if they don't need you, you'll find yourself with that free space to move forward with other tasks." And we both laughed.

In most jobs, it is practically impossible to have a set plan and follow it blindly. We are bombarded with interruptions or unforeseen events on a daily basis. There are intrinsic challenges within every job so, if we do not create space for them in our daily plan, we can end up being defeated by the workload tsunami.

Regardless of the situation in which you find yourself, even if you can't eliminate the problem completely, you can use small strategies to establish the much-needed barriers and thus put your health before your sense of responsibility. This particularly applies if you are fulfilling everything on the outside but you feel frustration or resentment inside.

When we do not set healthy limits we stop being consistent and in addition to putting our well-being at risk, we often find ourselves feeling so burned out that we eventually have no choice other than to resign.

Of course, sometimes we must (and want to) go above and beyond the call of duty to do a good job. Our contribution is essential for the entire team to move forward. The problem is not when we exert ourselves, but when it becomes overexertion which extends indefinitely, to our emotional detriment.

GO FOR IT

If you have already set limits but you still cannot keep your head above water it is time to act, by approaching whoever can help you or by taking the steps that are already in your hands to take care of your needs.

When there is good communication other important elements grow, such as trust, sincerity and respect. During childhood we learned to smother certain feelings and thoughts to avoid conflict. There are feelings that, if not expressed, give rise to all kinds of obstacles in a relationship: misunderstandings, frustrations, disappointments and, ultimately, a rift.

Being able to express ourselves honestly and without any emotional charge, is vital. This includes having the ability to openly ask for what we want. Others don't have a crystal ball, no matter how well they know us. It is essential that we don't give people the impression that we're just whining. We need to present our audience with a sufficiently argued and balanced case and not simply make a list of complaints whilst pointing the finger.

IF IT DOES NOT SERVE YOU, LET IT GO

⚠ THERE ARE, UNFORTUNATELY, SOME UNSUSTAINABLE SITUATIONS FOR WHICH THERE ARE NO RESOURCES NOR IS THERE THE NECESSARY DETERMINATION FOR POTENTIAL SOLUTIONS TO BECOME A REALITY.

⚠ WHEN WE ARE IN THIS SITUATION, WAITING INDEFINITELY FOR CIRCUMSTANCES TO CHANGE IS NAÏVE, TO SAY THE LEAST.

If what you need is not possible or simply does not happen, it is time to let go. For this, we must take a leap of faith and throw ourselves into the void. Uncertainty and new challenges can awaken an infinity of fears and sensations that had been hidden: the fear of not pleasing others or rejection; insecurity about showing ourselves as we are and saying what we think; doubts about what behaviours are appropriate; what others say and/or mean. A lot of emotions and thoughts do not appear when we are in an established relationship or project because the roles have already been cast and we have, rightly or wrongly, a clear interpretation of the shared environment; its values, rules and expectations.

Furthermore, it is difficult for us to let go of obsolete personal relationships or projects, perhaps because of the role that a person or enterprise has had in our lives; practical, physical or economic aspects; the fear of being alone; of being out of work, etc.

⚠ WAITING FOR OTHERS TO CHANGE IS NOT A STRATEGY THAT USUALLY LEADS TO RESULTS. WE ARE THE ONLY ONES WHO CAN CHANGE OUR BEHAVIOUR OR ATTITUDE.

When we have given all that we can to a relationship and we have done so with maturity and as an adult, if the job or the person does not give us what we need, the healthy option is to end it.

Separations can be very traumatic because usually, by the time they happen, mutual wounds can have been caused during the period of decline. If we can let go of relationships before entering that phase of swampy terrain, we can mutually avoid a lot of distress and the relationship is more likely to evolve into another, albeit a very different one, rather than ending altogether.

In my life I have closed many chapters of work and personal relationships, but none in which the door has been permanently closed. Lengthening outdated interactions is like being the last one to leave a party; it never leaves you with a good taste in your mouth.

If you have closed chapters or relationships in bad circumstances, or are living through a difficult situation, ask yourself:

- Have I taken care of my needs along the way?
- Have my expectations been realistic?
- Have I expressed my needs to those who can influence the situation?
- Have I explicitly asked for what I need?
- Have I been able to say no?

We are all human and constantly face situations that make us feel outside of our comfort zone, especially in relationships. Creating a Plan B is a good way forward when we do not know what to do, even if we are not yet ready to let go and bring things to an end. Ask yourself:

- Have I been waiting a long time for something to change, but without success?

For example, you may have been waiting for a promotion in your company for quite some time but which doesn't materialise or that your business never seems to turn a profit; a person you like doesn't appear to have even noticed you or that a relationship which used to be good has become toxic.

> [!] SOMETIMES WE ARE SO FOCUSED ON PLAN A THAT WE DON'T CONSIDER THERE IS AN ALTERNATIVE - PLAN B.

Some powerful questions we can ask ourselves are:

- What if I continue to pursue this goal without success?
- What won't happen if I continue to try unsuccessfully?
- What if I achieve it?
- What won't happen if I do achieve it?
- What's the worst thing that can happen if I do what I need to take care of myself?
- Can I imagine other outcomes?

These questions are like a cold shower which can wake us up and lead us to take charge of the situation.

Of course, it is good to have desires and pursue our dreams but when we are disengaged; when what we want and have worked towards fails to happen, it is preferable to pause, re-evaluate and seek an alternative that can lead us towards taking better care of ourselves.

To act decisively we need to be able to say 'no' to some things, even those things we deeply desire and have pursued with tenacity. Having a Plan B can help us change course and break into new territory where we might find wonderful things we'd never even considered before.

There are always new alternatives to explore, with the potential to generate new paths, even if they are not the specific dream we had. Ask yourself:

- Is it possible that I don't know what is in my best interest?

> [!] WE HAVE THREE CHOICES: TO MOVE FORWARD WITH NEW PROJECTS; TO STAY WHERE WE ARE BUT FEELING FRUSTRATED BY THE FEELING OF STAGNATION; OR TO SIMPLY ACCEPT OUR SITUATION AND PUT ALL HOPE FOR BETTERMENT OUT OF OUR MINDS.

There is no need to succumb to despair in the process!

> [!] WE ARE OUR OWN TRAVEL COMPANIONS, SO WHY NOT MAKE AN EFFORT TO TAKE CARE OF OURSELVES AND ACT CONSISTENTLY WITH OUR NEEDS.

No matter how fortunate we are in our projects, or that we have people who we love and value, the most important component in our lives is ourselves, so if you still haven't started treating yourself as your own best friend, what are you waiting for?

AND IF YOU CAN'T LET GO, THEN WHAT?

Having said all of this, it is not always appropriate to just take care our own needs and there are times when it is not feasible to let go. In those cases, we still have the ability to choose; maybe not the circumstances but our motivation so that we can ensure that our actions are consistent with our thoughts and feelings.

The first step is to identify our motivation in the fulfilment of our obligations. To do this you can ask yourself:

- Are my actions born out of freedom or fear?

Take the time to feel the emotion that drives your actions every day. There is no right answer, it is what it is! Once you have identified the emotion that feeds the fulfilment of your obligation, ask yourself:

- What brought me to this situation?

It may have fulfilled a wish you once had. For example, if you are now taking care of someone, you may have unconsciously decided to feel needed in your childhood. Or maybe that job that demands so much of you is bringing you the economic well-being you always wanted. Sometimes, we contradict ourselves by resenting fulfilled dreams.

Whether the situation is connected to a fulfilled wish or not, we have the freedom to choose the motivation that feeds our actions: from "I have to ..." to, "I choose to enjoy my fulfilled dream and accept that it entails ..." or, "I make a gift because I want to."

When we choose our motivation out of awareness and logic, the experience changes completely.

Score from 1 to 10 the statements below from two perspectives, how important they are to you, and the time and effort you devote to them, being 1 "Nothing" and 10 "A lot":

	Importance	Dedication
Advancing in my professional development		
Making more money		
Learning new capabilities		
Enjoying my work		
Having hobbies or areas of interest		
Having free time for myself		
Enjoying personal relationships		
Being fit		
Being healthy		

Write your own ideas and score them:

	Importance	Dedication
-		
-		
-		
-		
-		

- Identify the statements in which the level of importance you have given them is significantly higher than your level of dedication.
- Identify areas where your dedication is significantly greater how important they are.
- Write down what you have become aware of by doing this exercise.
- Summarise your thoughts and pick three things you'd like to do to find a better balance between what matters to you and your level of dedication.

Chapter 16

TAKE CARE OF YOUR HEALTH

DO YOU SUFFER FROM STRESS?

If you had asked me that a few years ago, I would have said no. However, every Friday afternoon my jaw hurt and, when I fell asleep, it closed with such force that the noise used to wake me up. Some time later, I was so exhausted that I experienced what we call burnout.

It is possible to be so focused on our external world without paying attention to our body that we do not notice the signs of stress that manifest in us, both physically and emotionally.

How does stress manifest itself in you? If you have an answer to this question, the good news is that knowing that you suffer from stress, it is in your power to mitigate or prevent it.

The causes of stress are complex and depend not only on what happens to us but on how we deal with things. Abandoning the factors that cause us stress is not always possible, nor is it the solution. Our well-being depends on being less reactive to what happens to us and taking steps to mitigate what is happening to us.

If you are one of those people who believe that you do not suffer from stress, you do not have anything to lose by observing yourself, just in case. When we pay attention to our body on a day-to-day basis, we can observe which specific situations increase our cortisol levels. Physical symptoms may present as: tension in the temple, back or neck; tightness in the chest; skin reactions; or changes in breathing, among others. In my case, when I started paying attention to my body, I clearly identified which situations caused the most reactivity in me and accentuated my physical response to stress.

Self-care is vital because the symptoms of stress can be the precursor of the dreaded burnout - when we have had enough, are demotivated and have little enjoyment of life.

And you may think, "Stress is a reality of the world we live in and it's not practical to try to avoid it."

> THINKING ABOUT WHAT A STRESS-FREE EXISTENCE MEANS TO US CAN HELP US GET CLOSER.

After having undertaken my personal discovery journey and made changes in my life, as I write these lines I am living an experience practically without stress. I come to this conclusion when I think about my physical health, work, environment, circumstances and, above all, my attitude.

At other times in my life, I chose confrontation to succeed, sought justice and always wanted to be right. Now I see the world from a different perspective, which I hope I have shared in part with you. From this new place I take care of myself, I do the things I really value and I choose my battles carefully - and when I choose to fight I do freely and not as the reaction by default.

> 💬 **WHEN WE SEE THE WORLD FROM A BROADER PERSPECTIVE, WE CAN MAKE RATIONAL DECISIONS AND CHOOSE WHICH BATTLES ARE WORTH FIGHTING.**

So, what does a stress-free life mean to me?

- Not having jaw pain on Fridays.
- Feeling free to change my plans, both in the workplace and in my private life; being able to improvise and do things that I haven't planned ahead.
- Making time for certain activities because I like them and they add value to my life, and not because I should do them.
- Making fewer plans for the future and enjoying uncertainty. This allows me to explore new opportunities which can surprise me, without the fear of not fulfilling a plan that existed only in my imagination.
- Taking naps, playing sports and enjoying nature.

And, above all, to carefully manage my thoughts when there are situations that challenge me and making the choice to live each day without stress, enjoying the trip, with potholes and everything.

Ask yourself and reflect:

- What would a life without (or with less) stress look like for me?
- How would I know I have achieved it?
- What activities would I spend time on?
- What difficult aspects would I leave behind?
- What elements that I value I would lose?
- What can I do to have less stress in my life?
- What can I stop doing to suffer less from stress?
- Make a list of simple things that would evidence that you don't suffer from stress.
- Write down what you have acknowledged by doing this exercise.
- Summarise your thoughts, selecting three things you would like to do to get closer to having a stress-free experience.

IDENTIFY YOUR HARMFUL BEHAVIOURS

> [!] STRESS HIDES BEHIND BEHAVIOURS WHICH, IF WE STOP TO QUESTION THEM, WARN US THAT SOMETHING IS NOT RIGHT.

One morning, I arrived at the office a little fuzzy from having a slight headache. I turned my computer on and, looking at my diary, I saw that it was full. It was going to be one of those days when I would even have a hard time finding time to go to the bathroom between meetings, although with a bit of luck I could nip to the canteen to buy lunch. I was a little slow and my temples hurt. Ouch! How hard Monday mornings are after having had a nice weekend with the family!

We had spent a nice Saturday dining with friends and walking our dog. Sunday had been quiet, at home, doing odd little chores around the house and then having a lovely Sunday lunch - one of those when you spend a couple of hours cooking and after eating it, you collapse on the sofa to spend the afternoon vegging. We had a superb wine with a delicious roast and, since we had nothing to do for the rest of the day, we said: "Let's open another bottle of wine to go with the cheese." Hence, we spent the afternoon in a state of drowsiness, with a half-watched movie and a little more wine, until the evening came and that familiar feeling of numbness arrived.

As on so many occasions, the weekend was over and ended with a headache and an uncomfortable, nervous feeling in my belly. At no point did I link it to the fact that something wasn't right. The following morning, I added that discomfort to the weight of my responsibilities and work demands: the emails that needed a response; the pressure from my superiors; and the challenges my department faced, adding to the situation my headache, dehydration and the inability to think with the clarity and agility that used to characterise me. And at no point did I think, "Here's something that doesn't add up, Susana." And I would think, "We didn't drink that much - a couple of bottles of wine between the two of us for the whole Sunday." When I think about it, I see that I went to the office too many times with a hangover and stupid excuses, without stopping to associate this behaviour with the general deterioration I had been suffering as a result of the work pressure and stress it caused me.

Now that I have learned to take care of myself and I have a hangover, at most, a couple of times a year, I realise that this behaviour caused me even more damage that I had ever imagined. The fact is that trying to keep up with the pace of my job was already causing me enough problems and I was then adding the physical and mental difficulties caused by my lack of rest. The problem was not so much the alcohol but the fact that when I drink wine I am unable to sleep well, so the next day I would arrive at the office exhausted, making the experience much harder. My rising stress levels were being aggravated by my own bad routine. I had not stopped to question the habit that always resulted in my feeling bad and although it was fun, it was no longer worth it. I had employed a number of strategies to ignore the situation because I knew that if I tried but failed to stop, I would end up with that sense of guilt we all feel when we are unable to stick to the resolutions we make. In short: a disaster. That was my harmful habit for a while.

> WE ALL HAVE, AT SOME POINT, HARMFUL HABITS THAT IMPACT OUR LIVES.

> THESE GUILTY PLEASURES TAKE THEIR TOLL ON US AND ELIMINATE OPPORTUNITIES TO ENJOY OR SUCCEED.

These routines feed on our negative thoughts and feelings, even if they appear to be positive from an outside perspective. In my case, I associated alcohol with social events and having fun, without realising that it was taking a massive toll on my life. Ask yourself:

- What habits do I have in my life that make me think and feel negatively?

Although the real question is:

- What negative thoughts and feelings are hidden behind this behaviour which isn't worth it?

> ⚠ BEHIND HARMFUL HABITS THERE ARE DEEP CAUSES OF DISSATISFACTION OR AVOIDANCE. IF WE DO NOT IDENTIFY THE SOURCE THAT FEEDS THESE NEGATIVE SENSATIONS, EVEN IF WE MANAGE TO CHANGE OUR BEHAVIOUR, WE WILL NOT HEAL THE UNDERLYING PROBLEM.

Ask yourself:

- What feeds my harmful habit?
- What am I avoiding or postponing?
- What situations make me want to continue to do this?

I remember a conversation with a colleague who had a video game addiction and talking about this topic. He came to the conclusion that part of the challenge was that he had to accept that in order to move forward, he had to abandon an activity that he really enjoyed. A key step in letting go of any habit or addiction is to acknowledge the grieving implicit in the acceptance that it is no good for you, and never will be, no matter how much we like it. Instead of ignoring our grief, we can feel it and let it run its course, to the point where we are able to turn the page by replacing old bad habits with new, healthy ones.

We have talked about stress and how, in avoiding habits that do not benefit us, we take care of our health. However, health encompasses much more than the absence of stress.

THE MIND FEEDS THE BODY

The well-known yoga guru, B. K. S. Iyengar, defined health as: 'A state of complete harmony of the body, mind and spirit. When one is free from physical disabilities and mental distractions.' Physical fitness, although not the solution to all our problems, in my case has been an important aspect of my well-being.

If you take care of your body and exercise regularly, although not obsessively, and you do it because you want to take care of yourself and not as an obligation – congratulations! I had never been one of those people but I have finally managed to put it into practice after years doing the opposite - giving priority to everything before my own physical well-being.

In addition to not prioritizing physical activity, my level of fitness was not good and, of course, the issue with lacking physical fitness is that it is a vicious circle. When we are not used to it the body suffers, we have difficulty breathing and our motivation is low. When we have little physical strength, as a result of our lifestyle and we add all of our responsibilities - our work, the endless list of tasks we haven't done, that last-minute problem that needs to be solved, the house, the children, our partner, parents - finding the time to exercise regularly is not easy.

I'm embarrassed to confess that I always used to schedule a yoga class or gym session on my company diary. Every year the proposed activity changed and I added sessions that I wanted to do, even just walking at lunch time. I scheduled them because I thought, "Well, if I put it on my diary, I'll do it." However, as my work schedule was constantly changing, any excuse or the slightest problem made me lower the priority level of the exercise compared to the other demands that were apparently unpostponable. The reality is that the decision is in our hands and that we choose to prioritise other responsibilities, not only because they have to be tackled at some stage but because, deep down, we feel lazy, discouraged or choose not to take care of ourselves enough.

I have always been mindful of my diet and weight. However, now that I am in better shape, I realise how abysmal my level of physical strength was.

⚠️ WHEN WE FIND OURSELVES IN A SUBOPTIMAL STATE OF HEALTH, WE GET USED TO IT AND DON'T NOTICE HOW POOR IT IS UNTIL WE EXPERIENCE SOMETHING DIFFERENT.

Once exercising became a part of my routine and not an occasional activity, I noticed that daily exercise is like an elixir. In my experience, it's not enough to exercise once a week if we want to see any real benefits. I consoled myself by thinking, "Well, at least I go for a walk every weekend." Well, no, it is not the same.

> WHEN WE ACT SENSIBLY, WE TAKE CARE OF OURSELVES TO FEEL GOOD PHYSICALLY AND THIS IS ACCOMPANIED BY A FEELING OF EMOTIONAL WELL-BEING AND GREATER RELAXATION.

> TO ACHIEVE THIS, IT IS NECESSARY TO CREATE THE HABIT OF LOVING OURSELVES AND EXERCISING REGULARLY AND IN A HEALTHY WAY.

Make sure the activity you choose fits into your life. For example, going from doing nothing to exercising for an hour three times a week is not realistic for everyone. Doing that usually results in our starting out with energy and good intentions but, after a few days or weeks, we return to our old routines and end up doing nothing.

When I began to listen to my body, I noticed the havoc that stress was having on me and realised that I needed to improve my health. After several attempts, I can now share with you the method that has helped me to finally stop procrastinating and improve my physical condition. It might help you too.

CREATE A HABIT

The first step was to become accustomed to it. If we do not create a routine, it is impossible for it to last, especially in the case of sport.

It takes effort to create the habit of exercising to strengthen our physique, and it is all too easy to lose that habit. Even in my case now, writing these pages and being in a pretty good physical condition, if I stop for only two weeks it is like reversing months of progress. Physical fitness is an ongoing commitment because if we don't keep it up, we lose our shape easily. But that is okay, as we will discuss in the third step, because it is about attitude.

> CREATING A HABIT MEANS FINDING A PLACE IN YOUR DAILY ROUTINE, IDEALLY EVERY DAY BUT AT LEAST 5 TO 6 DAYS A WEEK, RESERVING A SMALL SPACE FOR EXERCISING.

The forms are endless: walking, swimming, yoga - choose whatever suits you - but that space needs to be something fixed in your daily routine because if it isn't, it is easy for other demands to come and replace it. Creating a routine is easier when the activity happens at the same time each and every day. In my case, I do yoga in the morning. I know that if I do it just after I wake up, before doing absolutely anything, I do it and that's it. Whenever I try to do any other activity first, I lose the habit and I start convincing myself not to bother, by creating excuses. That is how the probability of not doing it at all multiplies.

I started exercising just ten minutes a day. I did yoga in the morning for ten minutes and I thought, "Hey-ho, ten minutes is better than nothing." And as time passed, those ten minutes kept growing because my body was getting stronger and so was my habit. For that reason, in my opinion, it is more productive to promise yourself to do ten minutes a day and keep it up, than to commit to doing an hour but then giving up.

> THE DIFFICULTY LIES IN TAKING THAT INITIAL STEP, LAYING DOWN THE MAT, GOING TO THE POOL OR WHATEVER THAT STEP IS, AS YOUR STARTING POINT.

I now usually have a longer routine, up to forty-five minutes to an hour. If one day I do not want to take that long, nothing bad happens, but I do my best to maintain those ten minutes.

> 🔲 **IF WE SET THE EXPECTATION LOW, TAKING THAT FIRST STEP WILL BE EASIER.**

Once we have crossed that initial barrier it is much easier to keep it going. Thus, we pave the way for that activity which eventually, instead of lasting for just few minutes, will last a little longer. Even if it is only ten minutes, those ten minutes are beneficial and the important thing is to maintain the habit.

TAKE CARE OF YOUR ATTITUDE

"Attitude is the brush with which the mind colours life. We choose the colours." (unknown) If we focus on the road ahead, from the poor physical condition we currently have, to where we would like to go, we can miss the signs of improvement along the way. For example, I remember when I started doing press-ups in yoga, when I lowered my body I was totally unable to do it slowly. My body would collapse. If at that moment I had said to myself, "How am I ever going to get down slowly, let alone get back up?" I'd have given up completely! If we only focus on the gap we have to narrow, it feels so wide that we become demotivated.

> 🔲 **IT IS IMPORTANT TO OBSERVE OUR PROGRESS, HOWEVER SMALL. NOT TO OBSESS ABOUT WHERE WE WANT TO GO OR WHERE WE THINK WE SHOULD BE, BUT TO CELEBRATE THE TREND OF IMPROVEMENT WE OBSERVE.**

If we create the habit sustainably, it is easier than we think. You will notice significant physical improvement quite quickly. It will help if you concentrate on the upwards trend and celebrate it. It's futile to blame ourselves or feel bad for not being at the level our mind tells us we should be.

Small improvements can be very rewarding. I remember one morning when, after six months of trying to learn how to make a Shirshasana, I managed to do it without leaning on the wall for the first time.

This yoga pose involves standing upside down with the weight on your forearms and head. Pretty easy for some, but not for me. I had been doing yoga for two years and learning this posture had more to do with my willpower and facing my fears than with my physical ability.

If I had known that I would need six months of almost daily practice to learn, I probably wouldn't have even started. We are naturally so impatient that if we are not able to achieve the goals we set for ourselves quickly, sometimes we do not even try.

My path in this process taught me something. My experience was made up of small but steady victories. When I started, I was aware that this was not going to be easy for me and for that reason I loved noticing every little step of my improvement.

Every day the tiniest sign of progress was enough for me so the process, instead of being full of frustration, was full of enjoyment. What a difference attitude makes! Instead of reproaching myself for being so slow, I congratulated myself for having the patience and willpower to keep going. The deep sense of pride and satisfaction I felt cannot be achieved with any quick results.

I may never get to perfect this pose, but it doesn't matter. What I learned from this is that if we remove the sense of urgency when we try to achieve what we seek, in addition to getting there we can savour the process at every step. Even if we do not achieve a goal perfectly, we can gain satisfaction if we are able to appreciate the improvements made, however small they may be.

When you are in the middle of a big challenge, whether it's related to physical exercise or not, ask yourself:

- What small improvements can I observe?

The attitude we need includes not beating ourselves up if, on one occasion, we don't stick to the routine we planned. It is not about brow-beating ourselves; it is about having patience, treating ourselves kindly, recognising that we all have good days and bad days, and that the important thing is that although one day you may not have stuck with your routine, the next day you will. That's the attitude that fuels the process of maintaining a healthy habit.

Finally, it is important to take that behaviour wherever we go, including on vacation and business trips. When we break a routine we can easily lose it. According to University College London, to create a habit we need between 18 and 254 days. Regardless of how much we need to create it, it takes much less time to lose it, so looking for strategies to maintain that habit, even if it is not 100 per cent perfect, is important. For example, when I go on a trip I always pack my yoga mat.

If you want to create a habit of regular exercise, reflect and write:

- At what time of day could you regularly spare 15 minutes?
- Create a list of physical exercise ideas that do not require preparation time before (or clearing-up time after) the activity.
- Write about the barriers that stand in your way of creating your healthy habit.
- What can you do to remove those barriers?
- Write about the resources you have to create that new behaviour.
- What will happen if you can't do it?
- What will happen if you manage it?

- How are you going to reward yourself if you do it?
- Summarise in a few words your proposal to create a habit of exercising regularly.

FIND YOUR OWN WAY

After all the questions you have asked yourself during this self-reflection journey, and now that it is coming to an end, there is a question that is important and to which only you will have the answer. Ask yourself:

- What does success mean for me?

CHOOSE YOUR WISHES AGAIN

One definition of triumph is to be victorious, to succeed in an endeavour.

> ⚠️ EACH CULTURE HAS A DIFFERENT UNDERSTANDING OF WHAT IT MEANS TO TRIUMPH OR TO SUCCEED AND IT IS POSSIBLE TO FIND ADDITIONAL INTERPRETATIONS IN EACH FAMILY SETTING.

There are families in which the 'god of money' is worshipped. In others, it's the god of work, the god of marriage, or even the god of culture. It is interesting to look at our own family experiences – the ethos of our parents - to compare their ways of thinking and comparable values within other family systems. Let's look at my family: both of my parents were entrepreneurs

and we lived comfortably. I now realise that in my home it was the god of work who was worshipped.

My parents worked a lot and didn't usually take holidays. As a child, I didn't have the experience of a family vacation. Our 'family-time' happened during the weekend, for example, going out to eat. My parents have always encouraged me to work hard. In fact, even at my age, every time I have a conversation with my mother, if I pay attention I notice that she talks to me about work and its importance. She pats me on the back, saying how hard I try and how proactive I am. In this cult of the god of work, success means achieving things through our work and anyone who does not is considered a failure. I am not sharing this as a criticism or complaint, but as an example for you to compare it with other systems that you have observed or experienced.

In contrast, in other family environments the 'god of education' is worshipped and the academic awards obtained by family members are the most important accolade. Their way of assessing whether or not they have done well in life is through the level of education achieved. Those who did not go to university are pitied because they are seen as a failure, while those who got first class honours are respected.

When we question the ways of interpreting success, it is clear that these ideas are as incomprehensible as they are wrong. All the gods are equally important in the right measure and, at the same time, useless. However, becoming aware of which god we idolise can be liberating, because we can thus decide, in an objective way, whether the goals promoted by the cult we are a part of are still worth pursuing or not.

It is useful to stop to think and ask ourselves: what does this god whom we worship provide for me?

Other more important questions are:

- What opportunity am I missing by adoring this god?
- What am I missing out on by proactively pursuing work, money, a partner, culture, academic achievement, status or anything else?

Every decision and action in life carries an 'opportunity cost', which is what we do not have or cannot achieve when we pursue our chosen path. The opportunity cost is not always easy to recognise.

Rate from 1 to 10 the following descriptions or expressions of what it means to succeed, with 1 being "Completely false" and 10 "Totally true":

Success is...

	Score
Achieving a high level of status	
Making a lot of money	
Getting to the top of my organisation	
Being respected by the people around me	
Affording a nice house with a garden	
Having a good car, the latest tech gadgets and quality possessions	
Sending my children to a private school	
Having the freedom to express myself	
Sleeping well at night	
Being able to pick up my children from school	
Having enough money to not worry about basic needs	
Being free to improvise	
Having the time for activities I like	
Not suffering from stress	

Add 5 additional things that are symbols of success for you:

-
-
-
-
-

- Identify which god of success is given the most importance in your family system.
- Do you pursue the values of your family system? If the answer is no, which symbol of success have you chosen?
- Which gods are idolised by the people around you?
- Write down what you've noticed by doing this exercise or any other observation that is relevant.

Think about the five things you chose as definitions of triumph for you:

- Write about what you lose by pursuing them, that is, the opportunity cost of each one?
- With the 10 things you have listed, five that represent success and five that represent what we lose by getting it, score them in order of importance with 1 being the least important thing for you and number 10 the most important.

Your 5 symbols of success:

Score

-
-
-
-
-
-

Your 5 opportunity costs:

Score

-
-
-
-
-
-

- Write down what you have become aware of by doing this exercise.
- Write about what you propose to do differently, if anything, after doing this exercise.

The above exercise is intended to help you explore the fact that, in reality, there is no single interpretation of success because even the most desired achievement takes its toll on us in some way.

In a casual conversation, I told one person, "I'm not willing to sell my life." He looked at me in surprise and repeated the phrase I had just said. I had said it without thinking, as part of the conversation, but his reaction made me spend time reflecting on what I had really meant. What did I mean by, "I'm not willing to sell my life"? It is a complex notion: time, dreams, experiences. People, without realising it, can exchange those things for the work we think we have to do, taking on responsibilities that we think we have to assume, pleasing others and trying to comply with the generally accepted rules dictated by the system we are part of. What I had wanted to express with that phrase is that I had come to realise that I had spent too much effort, time and energy letting myself be carried away by the rollercoaster ride I had been on - a treadmill of professional development towards earning a good salary and having prestige, amongst other things. I could now see that really, to have all those returns, I had been selling my life, accepting the opportunity cost that those decisions entailed.

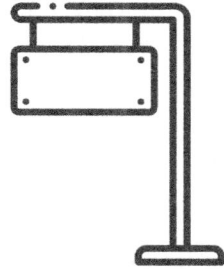

> ⚠ WITHOUT REALISING, WE EXCHANGE OUR LIVES FOR THE THINGS WE WANT TO ACHIEVE, ACCEPTING THE OPPORTUNITY COST THAT THOSE DECISIONS ENTAIL.

When we begin to identify what we are missing out on, it is easier to know which way to go, just as sometimes it is easier to know what we do *not* want than what we *do* want. However, there is a subtle but important difference; we have to be sure that our aversion is not fuelled by our fears.

In conclusion, it is interesting to acknowledge the price we pay by pursuing our dreams, goals or whatever we set out to do. That is why we could say that when we choose our job, we are selling the time we have.

For this reason, I encourage you to question yourself:

- Am I selling my life?
- What do I lose when I make decisions each day about what I spend my time on?
- And what do I receive in return?

Because when what we get back does not compensate for what we miss out on, maybe it is time to rethink.

YOU ONLY LIVE ONCE

For a brief moment I did not remember the events of the last three days. I had that feeling we have when waking up naturally on a Saturday morning - that cosy and lazy drowsiness when we know we are awake but not in a hurry to open our eyes and make it official. Does that sound familiar?

Suddenly, a jolt of alarm invaded my body. Reality hit me and the blissful few seconds I had just felt vanished. It wasn't Saturday nor was I in my bed. My throat hurt and I couldn't swallow.

I opened my eyes, disoriented. I saw the ceiling. It was one of those that resembles a chess board with squares perfectly ordered and supported by thin metal grids. Every three or four sections included a water sprinkler or an air conditioning grille.

The pain in my throat worsened; it was a sharp and stiff pain. In an involuntary reflex I tried for the thousandth time to swallow what blocked my throat, worsening the situation because my inability to breathe only added to my pain. I felt fear.

Noticing that I was going into a panic loop, I said to myself, "Susana, calm down, you can breathe. You only have to relax and stop swallowing. Come on you can do it!"

Soon after, I had regained my composure and felt throughout my body the well-being that this small change of attitude had in me. "Well done!" I said to myself.

When my attention moved away from the pain in my throat, my very next thoughts were work-related; "I have deadlines," "I have a presentation to give," "I can't let my colleagues down," etc. I had almost died hours before and there I was, thinking about the bloody office.

I was such a dedicated career woman that not taking care of my work responsibilities was unthinkable. On the bright side, at least what happened gave me a free pass to take a well-deserved rest. I had been carrying an unbearable workload. With a little luck I would be away for a couple of weeks.

The nurse came up to my bed, which drew my attention to the sound of the machine that was measuring my vital signs and the cannula in my arm to keep me free of pain.

"Hello, Susana, how are you?" He greeted me cheerfully as he went about carrying out all his checks. I raised my right hand and, unable to vocalise, I smiled to answer that well. "My name is Vicente and I am here for whatever you need. It seems that everything has gone well during the operation. The surgeon will come by in a while to see you, now you're awake."

The intensive care room could be seen almost entirely from where I was. There was one other patient at the end of the room, on the left. And, although I couldn't see it, the nurses' station was to my right. I could hear the conversation between Vicente and his colleague perfectly well. For hours they talked cordially about all kinds of topics; about their partners, the homemade cake someone had brought from home, of the indignation of the ward staff with the shifts assigned that week. And also, of course, COVID-19.

"I am so thirsty!" I thought. My mouth was dry despite the drip and I would have given anything to be able to brush my teeth!

Luckily, being a privately owned hospital at the beginning of the pandemic, they still did not treat COVID patients. The nurse told Vicente about the challenging conditions in which she had worked at another hospital which did accept COVID patients - the preparation protocol before each shift, how hot she felt under the protective gear, the lack of respirators, the people who were dying.

Just two weeks earlier, life seemed normal and with the certainties that we like to imagine. And there I was, in the middle of a pandemic, recovering from a major operation with a new scar 25 centimetres long.

A few days earlier I had been working harder than ever, supporting the business to manage the challenges caused by the pandemic whilst suffering from pains in my belly, albeit without paying much attention to them, until eventually the pain was stronger than I was and I had no choice but to go to the emergency room. The cause turned out to have been a serious intestinal obstruction, resulting in the operation which was now forcing me to put my life on hold.

My mind was wandering again; it was going back to the office. The anaesthetics seemed to be subsiding and, as it slowly faded away, I felt a sly little twinge in my belly; half pain, half nausea. It was a physical feeling and, at the same time, emotional discomfort. They say we have a second brain in the gut.

And suddenly I knew. I saw it clearly. I had one of those moments of absolute clarity. It was not that I wanted to have a break; it was that I didn't want to go back at all. As soon as the agony of the last few days seemed to have passed, I said to myself, "If I get out of this one, enough! Enough of doing what I am supposed to do, being so responsible, working so hard, to make more money than I need - to prove something. To prove what? Prove what to whom?"

In that moment of total surrender and vulnerability, the only thing I wanted was to have the nasogastric tube removed so that I could breathe. My precious work suddenly seemed a triviality. My profession, which I had enjoyed and which had motivated me, seemed redundant and felt as unnecessary in my life as that tube now was in my oesophagus. Suddenly my life - and time, precious as it is - seemed too valuable not to spend it doing what I now wanted.

Now. Not tomorrow. Not next year!

Since that day in the ICU, I have made many changes including using my experience as an executive to write this book and become a mentor to professionals and entrepreneurs - a professional role that I enjoy every day.

I have felt fear and had doubts along the way but that moment in the ICU has been my greatest ally - that moment of absolute clarity which put everything into perspective. Every decision I now make, I decide from a different perspective, creating space to live – LIVE in capital letters – no longer using a wrist watch, enjoying new discoveries such as mountain biking, traveling the planet and savouring the simple things that amaze me every day.

So now that our exploration journey together comes to an end, it is time to part company and send you on your way. I hope you have enjoyed it. My parting advice to you is:

Pursue your ambitions, enjoy growing, get to know yourself and do not forget about the person that you are in your pursuit. And when something inside tells you that it is time to change, that something is outdated, take the necessary steps and start again.

It's okay to have ambitions and pursue them, but you only live once. Life is like a book, full of chapters - episodes that may follow a specific plot but of which we are the authors.

When we have one of those moments of absolute clarity that we all encounter along the way, we are free to question the beliefs we inherited, change our priorities and give a good twist to the book we are writing, to live the story that unfolds in front of us, not the one we thought we were going to live.

So here I leave you with my final question for you:

What story are *you* going to write?

I hope you have enjoyed this manual and that you will come back to it in the future when you want to refresh the strategies that, with its help, you have defined by yourself.

If you would like to find out more about my offering and the Bonus available to those who have read this book, visit: **www.serranodavey.com/readers**.

Do remember that it can be a great gift for that person you have thought of as you read it.

In any case, you can subscribe to my mailing list at **www.serranodavey.com** so I can continue to help you and keep you informed.

You can also feel free to write to me at **susana@serranodavey.com** with any positive or constructive comment you may want to make. I would love to receive your feedback after having talked so much about it on the book.

Thank you for you time.

BIBLIOGRAPHY

This book contains my learnings and the methods I have developed to organise my recommendations. These learnings would not have been possible without the contribution of all the people who have accompanied me along the way. I have also relied on 'bites', as we do in food tasting, of some theories greatly developed by experts in their fields. So here is a bibliography that can guide you if you want to explore in more detail some of the ideas of others that I have presented.

- Bandler, R. & Grinder, J. (2005). The structure of magic. Science and Behaviour Books.
- Cameron, J. (2020). *The artist's way: a spiritual path to higher creativity.* Souvenir Press.
- Gallup. (2022). *Strengthsfinder 2.0.* Gallup Press.
- John C. Maxwell (2006). T*he 360 Degree Leader Workbook: Developing your Influence from Anywhere in the Organisation.* HarperChristian Resources.
- Hawkins, D. R. (2014). *Letting go: the pathway of surrender.* Hay House Inc.
- Naranjo, C. (2012). *27 personajes en busca del ser.* The key.
- Ruiz, M. (1997). *The Four Agreements: A practical guide to personal freedom. Amber-Allen Publishing, Incorporated.*
- Torres, S. (2017). *A bridge to reality.* Uranus.
- Yllengar, B.K.S. (2013). *The Tree of Yoga: The Definitive Guide to Yoga in Everyday Life.* Harper Collins.